## Nice People Dancing to Good Country Music
"Written with...deft comic assurance."—*Bay Guardian After Dark*

"Hilarious and affectionate..."—*Minneapolis Star and Tribune*

## Independence
"Powerful and thought-provoking." *Bristol* (R.I.) *Phoenix*

"Blessing is probing classic American psychodrama here, boldly facing the horrors of the devouring parent and the anguish of the struggling child....The play is at once repelling and fascinating."—*San Diego Union*

## Riches
"It's one kind of play by which theatre exists. It is so recognizably, so inescapably full of true life that, walking away at last, you may feel changed by the experience."—*Sacramento Bee*

"Blessing gives us two enormou~~s~~' in a turbulent moment of self-d *Journal*

D1464545

"Sharp and realistic."—*The Denv*

## Eleemosynary
"Blessing's finest work, an enriching tale of sin, regret and forgiveness."—William A. Henry III, *Time Magazine*

"There is a tart whimsicality to Lee Blessing's *Eleemosynary*, a zest for people who pursue their wayward idiosyncrasies..."—John Simon, *New York Magazine*

*About the Author:* Lee Blessing's best known play, *A Walk in the Woods*, has played on Broadway, throughout the United States, and with Sir Alec Guinness in London's West End. It has been performed in numerous other countries, including the Soviet Union, and was presented on PBS's "American Playhouse." The play received nominations for the Tony and Olivier awards, and won the American Theater Critics Award, among others. Besides the plays in this collection, Blessing has written *Cobb, Down the Road, Two Rooms,* and *Oldtimers Game* during the 1980s. Many of his plays have premiered at the Yale Repertory Theatre and the La Jolla Playhouse, where he has enjoyed strong working relationships with directors Lloyd Richards and Des McAnuff. Blessing has been awarded playwriting grants by the National Endowment for the Arts and the Guggenheim, Bush, McKnight, and Jerome foundations. He lives and works in his native Minneapolis with director Jeanne Blake.

# LEE BLESSING

# *F*OUR PLAYS

*e Dancing to
ntry Music*

*endence*

*ches*

*synary*

/METHUEN

ERRATUM

Lee Blessing: Four Plays (ISBN 0-435-08601-4)

Because of an error in printing, the contents of pages 39 and 40 were printed in the wrong order: the text of page 40 belongs on page 39, and the text of page 39 belongs on page 40.

**Heinemann Educational Books, Inc.**
*361 Hanover Street*
*Portsmouth, NH 03801-3959*
*Offices and agents throughout the world*

**Methuen Ltd.**
*Michelin House*
*81 Fulham Road*
*London SWI GRB*

*Nice People Dancing to Good Country Music* and *Toys for Men*, appearing here as one two-act play, ©1982 and 1983 separately by Lee Blessing. *Independence* ©1983 by Lee Blessing as an unpublished dramatic composition and again in 1985. *Riches* ©1986 by Lee Blessing as *War of the Roses*. *Eleemosynary* ©1987 by Lee Blessing.

Note: *Riches* was originally titled *War of the Roses*; the title was changed to avoid confusion with the motion picture. *Nice People Dancing to Good Country Music* and *Toys for Men* are published here as one full-length play, according to Lee Blessing's wishes.

**Library of Congress Cataloging-in-Publication Data**

Blessing, Lee.
[Plays. Selections]
Lee Blessing; four plays/Lee Blessing.
p. cm.
Contents: Nice people dancing to good country music—
Independence—Riches—Eleemosynary.
ISBN 0-435-08601-4
I. Title.
PS3552.L43A6    1990
812'.54—dc20                                                        90-38989
                                                                            CIP

**SPECIAL NOTES ON SONGS AND RECORDINGS:** For performance of such songs and recordings mentioned in these plays as are in copyright, the permission of the copyright owners must be obtained; or other songs and recordings in the public domain substituted.

Series design and cover by Jenny Greenleaf.
Printed in the United States of America
91  92  93  94  95      10  9  8  7  6  5  4  3  2  1

# CONTENTS

❖

# INTRODUCTION

❖

The four plays collected here were written consecutively, and were the first of mine to contain women. In the early 1980s, it seemed to me some of the most highly esteemed playwrights in America were men known for *not* writing important women characters into their plays. Articles by and about these writers appeared, reflecting neutrally or even positively on this absence in their work. While I doubt any signals had been sent intentionally, the subtle message male playwrights were receiving seemed clear enough: it was not crucial to learn how to write convincing women. I'm not certain things have changed a lot since then. Plays without significant women are still praised far more often than plays without significant men. Perhaps it's only natural that a society which so often suppresses real women will suppress fictional ones as well.

Still it seems unadventurous at the least for a man to avoid ever putting women at the center of a play—a little like trying to speak English without one of the parts of speech. In my own case I decided to make myself some "assignments"—plays which revolved around women. Inevitably I discovered that once you attempt to look at the world through the eyes of the other sex— no matter how imperfectly—you see a very different world. The moment my writing left the realm of the exclusively male, many simple and rigid "certainties" began to disappear for me, and were replaced by something far more *un*certain and rewarding— opening into the future, I thought, instead of the past.

The first of these plays was *Nice People Dancing to Good Country Music*. It began as a sort of fond tribute to some good ol' boy comedies. However it quickly shifted into a good ol' girl comedy (even if one was a recycled northerner with a borrowed accent and the other a former novice). The issues of dating, relationships and parenting all suddenly had to be viewed from the other side. While the play's not particularly serious in content, it did mark the first time I'd created women characters, and both were rebelling. Eve left her dull husband and their fifteen-year-old boy in St. Paul to begin a new life with an ex-biker running a bar in Houston. She didn't reject marriage—even her own— and motherhood so much as admit the fact that she was done with these things, and needed to move on. Her unrelenting self-satisfaction with her actions becomes for me the play's thematic motor. And the work of the play lies in her effort to bring her niece to see that living one's life is an utterly personal responsibility.

The weight that family brings to bear on the development of a young woman was dealt with far more seriously in my next play, *Independence*. This play began as a one-act about three sisters in Iowa, and gradually grew to full length with the inclusion of their mother, Evelyn. Many plays have explored the raw, archetypal struggle between fathers and sons. Fewer have suggested the relationship between a mother and daughter can be just as elemental, albeit often on different terms. In *Independence* I discovered three women who cannot completely become sisters until each comes to terms with what it means to be Evelyn's daughter. Women are asked to carry a disproportionate sense of responsibility for the integrity of families—even those into which they are simply born. For many women (and certainly those in this play) just "taking off" is not a satisfactory answer. Again and again, they find themselves drawn back to meet a crisis, to support a weak sibling, to tacitly ratify that the family itself—no matter how dangerous it might be for them— is valuable at all costs. "Independence" is exactly what's at stake.

*Riches* (formerly *War of the Roses*) is a treatise on marriage— the first time I chose this subject. The play has only two characters—husband and wife—and its action is initiated when

Carolyn suddenly confronts David (during what seems to be an idyllic anniversary weekend in the middle of the country in the middle of a marriage) with a problem he never knew existed. The remainder of the play consists of his struggle to understand, and her struggle to explain, what has gone wrong. Interestingly, I think Carolyn and David know far less about themselves and each other (in terms of their relationship) than do the women in *Independence*. It is only recently that the Riches have begun to realize how ingeniously they've hidden from one another. What they have to learn is that their problem is to discover not how to relieve pain, but how to feel it.

The final play in this group, *Eleemosynary*, is in many ways the airiest, the most celebratory. It follows the lives of a woman, her daughter and granddaughter from 1910 to the early 1980s. As with *Independence*, it's a world exclusively of women; not that there aren't men in their lives—only that the focus of *these* women is clearly and powerfully on themselves and each other. In this way, it differs a little I think from the other three plays. For while each woman suffers, and has suffered, at the hands of the other two, each also loves and reveres her position in the generational relationship. The pain here is leavened somehow— perhaps with a learned capacity to forgive those special blind- nesses and deafnesses which seem to accompany only the closest of our relationships.

No introduction for these plays could be complete without mention of the person with whom I was forming the most important love relationship of my life during the very years I wrote them. Jeanne Black dramaturged and/or directed each of these plays, and was intimately involved in the development of each of them. Not one of them would have been the same—some of them might not have existed—without her contribution. Nor would I be the same playwright. I'd be a different playwright— less interesting, I think. At least to me.

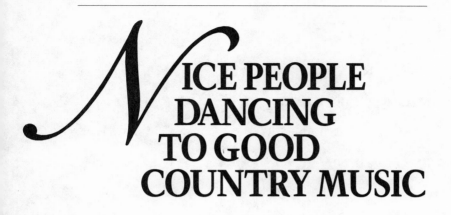

# NICE PEOPLE
# DANCING
# TO GOOD
# COUNTRY MUSIC

❖

*A Play in Two Acts*

# CHARACTERS

JIM STOOLS. . . . . . . . . . . . . . .41, bar owner, former biker

ROY MANUAL. . . . . . . . . . . . . . . . . . . . . .30, bar patron

JASON (JAY BOB) WILFONG. . . . . . .15, a summer guest

CATHERINE EMPANGER. . . . . . . . . . . . . .22, a novice

EVE (EVA JUNE) WILFONG. . . . . . . .38, Catherine's aunt

# TIME

The present, one morning in September

# PLACE

The Nice People Bar in Houston, Texas

# ACT ONE

*A parking lot. In it is the pickup truck of Jim Stools.*
*It points slightly up right. To Stage Right, the facade*
*and front door of the bar. The truck is at least fifteen*
*years old, battered, dirty, exhausted-looking. The*
*hood is up. Jim is working on the engine. He is*
*powerfully-built, wearing low-riding jeans and a*
*black T-shirt. He works quickly, almost feverishly.*
*As he works he hums along — in a frustrated, gutteral*
*sort of way — with the truck radio, which is playing*
*a kitschy version of "Deep In The Heart Of Texas."*\*

JIM. (*Humming, as he strains to turn a bolt and fails.*)
Shoot. (*He tries again, still humming, fails again. He strikes*
*the engine hard twice with the wrench. The radio cuts out.*)
Dammit. (*He tries a third time, strains as he hums, fails*
*again, hits the engine with the wrench again. The radio*
*comes on again.*) You son of a bitch, you're just toying with
me, ain't you? (*Tries once again, quickly, fails.*) Damn you,
can't you see I'm in a hurry?! (*He starts for the back of the*
*truck, striking the fender idly with his wrench. The radio cuts*
*out.*) Dammit. (*Speaking to the truck as he reaches the flat-*
*bed.*) I once saw a man eat a truck. Know that? Saw it on one
of them You Asked For It So You're Gonna Get It shows.
They had real film footage of a man eating a Ford Econoline,

\*See special note on copyright page.

3

piece by piece. (*Picking up a large tire iron from the back of the truck.*) Bit by bit he downed that sucker, all the way from the luggage rack right on down to the tires. Even ate the flashlight in the glove compartment. (*Moving once again to the front of the truck, brandishing the tire iron.*) Took him eleven years, but he did it. Food for thought. (*He addresses the problem bolt once more, carefully aligns the tire iron to it, then strikes it viciously several times. The radio comes on. He strikes once more. The radio cuts out.*) There. Have I got your attention now? (*Jim tries the bolt again. It turns with relative ease. Jim smiles and begins to work quickly again. Roy Manual enters from the bar, R. He is not large. He smiles almost constantly. His clothes suggest a hard worker, but with one or two gestures toward the image of the urban cowboy — dress shirt, dirty jeans, work boots.*)

ROY. Hey Jim? Jim?

JIM. Thought I asked you to watch the bar for me, Roy.

ROY. Oh, there ain't nobody in there. Say, Jim — I got a question.

JIM. Go away, Roy.

ROY. It's just a little question.

JIM. (*Still working.*) Go *away*, Roy.

ROY. See, all I want to know is . . .

JIM. Roy! Will you leave me alone? I'm trying to prevent a murder!

ROY. A murder?

JIM. Yeah, a murder. And I can't prevent it, 'less I get this miserable mother truck of mine moving — so go away!

ROY. Who's gonna get murdered?

JIM. (*As he works.*) Damn truck. Electrical problems. *Electrical* problems! You can't see 'em, can't trace 'em — you touch the wrong thing and you shock the living . . . (*He receives a shock.*) Aaaagh! *Damn* it! (*He works.*)

ROY. Who's gonna get murdered?

JIM. A kid, dammit, ok? A young boy's gonna die unless I

save him. Now go on and leave me alone.

ROY. Well sure, Jim . . . I didn't know, is all. Where is the boy, anyway?

JIM. (*Pointing violently off R.*) Right in there!

ROY. But . . . that's the bar, Jim. That's your own . . . (*Realizes.*) You mean little Jay Bob?

JIM. I mean little Jay Bob.

ROY. Who's gonna murder him?

JIM. Me, dammit! Me! If I can't get out of here in about one more minute.

ROY. But he's just a kid. What'd he do to . . . ?

JIM. (*Looking up.*) Just a kid, huh? You ain't had to live with him all summer. Oh, you should've heard Eva June last spring, "He's fifteen years old, he can help around the place." Help! Takes that boy a day to do a job that'd take a chimpanzee ten minutes. If I tell him to go get more beer glasses, I got a guaranteed two-hour wait. If I just leave him alone, he eats up every sour cream 'n onion potato chip in the place—and that's when he's not out back breaking full bottles of beer just for fun. Hell, it's got to where I give him any pointless job I can think of now, just to keep him busy. (*Receives a shock from the truck.*) Aaaagh!! *Shoot!*

ROY. Why are you mad at him today?

JIM. I caught him burning money.

ROY. Burning money? His money?

JIM. *My money!* Outta the till.

ROY. Well, how much did he . . . ?

JIM. Not much. I caught him when he was still working on the ones. (*Finishes on the engine.*) There. Let's see if it starts. (*Turns the key, gets nothing but a click.*) Damn!

ROY. (*As Jim returns to the engine and probes.*) Didn't work, huh? Well, that's electricity for you.

JIM. (*Receiving a bigger shock.*) Aaaaagh!!! *You damn thing! You damn, damn thing!!*

ROY. Hey, easy, Jim!

JIM. I don't want to kill anybody!

ROY. Well you don't *have* to . . .

JIM. I got to! Lend me your truck.

ROY. It's in the shop.

JIM. In the shop?! Well—*get* me a truck!

ROY. There ain't any. It's morning. Nobody comes to a bar in the morning.

JIM. You do.

ROY. Look, can't you just sit down with Jay Bob and talk?

JIM. You can't talk with a dead kid. Which is what he's gonna be if I get near him. Oh, *damn!!* (*Jim kicks the truck viciously. The radio comes on, playing "I Got A Never-Ending Love For You."\* Jim kicks it again. The radio cuts out. He sits on a fender, dispirited.*) You don't know what it's been like.

ROY. Well, when's he supposed to leave, anyway? I thought he was just here for the summer.

JIM. He is. He goes home tomorrow—to start torturing his father again.

ROY. Tomorrow? Hell, that ain't so bad.

JIM. It's twenty-four hours. You ever tried to hold a sneeze for twenty-four hours?

ROY. No.

JIM. That's how it feels. Not killing him. Feels just like I got a natural urge and I got to force myself not to fulfill it. It feels awful. (*He goes back under the hood.*)

ROY. So you're just going to drive away?

JIM. That's right.

ROY. Where?

JIM. Up and out. Just up onto the highway and out as far as I gotta go. That kid's cost me plenty of extra miles this summer.

ROY. How far . . . out do you go?

*See special note on copyright page.

6

JIM. Last time was to San Antone.

ROY. San Antone? That's 200 miles.

JIM. Can't help it. Got to keep going till the urge passes. Otherwise, I'll kill Eva June's son, and I can't do that. Never get involved with a woman who has kids, Roy.

ROY. Ok.

JIM. If you do, you'll be driving all over Texas. (*Hits the truck with the wrench.*) But not in this trash heap. Lump of garbage shaped like a truck! No woman is worth it, Roy. Believe me. No matter how much pleasure you draw from a woman, it ain't worth two minutes with a mean kid. (*Roy nods.*) I tried to be good to him. I did. I fixed his name — you know that? First thing, the minute he showed up. His real name is Jason, do you believe that? *Jason?* I practically vomited the first time I heard it. So I made up Jay Bob on the spot and gave it to him free of charge. Did he thank me? No way. Should've known right then he wasn't gonna work out. (*Jim works.*)

ROY. I'm sorry, Jim. I really am.

JIM. Thanks. Go away.

ROY. (*Watchng a moment.*) Say Jim, you remember that question I was asking you?

JIM. Question?

ROY. You know. I said I had a question?

JIM. Well what is it?

ROY. You remember that woman that Eva June brought through the bar with her about an hour ago? You know, just before Eva June went out?

JIM. Yeah?

ROY. Who was she?

JIM. Who was she. She's another one of Eva June's damn relatives, that's who she is. Some kinda niece or something. God knows how long she's planning to stay. One after another they come down here — just one after another, I tell you.

ROY. (*Smiling.*) Eva June's niece, huh? That's great.

JIM. How come?

ROY. That means she'll be around for awhile.

JIM. What's on your mind, Roy?

ROY. Nothing. I just like her, that's all.

JIM. You like her?

ROY. Yeah.

JIM. You only saw her for three seconds before she went upstairs.

ROY. I know, but I really like her. What's her name?

JIM. I ain't got time for this. I got a truck to fix.

ROY. I just want to get to know her better.

JIM. She ain't interested in you. She's interested in me.

ROY. In you? What for?

JIM. She's here to check me out. Eva June's whole damn family's been doing it: coming down here one by one from Minnesota to look me over and then report back to Command Central, or whatever it is.

ROY. Well, I guess that's . . . understandable, seeing as you stole Eva June away from her husband.

JIM. What's wrong with that?

ROY. Nothing. Just a fact.

JIM. The best man won. Hell, it's what America's all about: comparison shopping.

ROY. I know. I got no objection.

JIM. Wasn't like I set out to steal her. Our luggage got tangled up in a metal detector at the Dallas Airport. We started talking, that's all. By the time we got out to the end of the concourse, we were in love. 'Least, I was. She must've liked it ok, too, though. She changed her reservation.

ROY. (*With admiration.*) I love that story. Wish that could happen to me with a woman.

JIM. Well, it ain't no use, 'less she's a woman without relatives. (*Gets another shock.*) Damn! This thing's alive, I swear it. I'm gonna sneak up on it. (*He goes underneath the truck.*)

8

ROY. Electricity's one of the mysteries of the Earth, ain't it?

JIM. Shut up and get me that tire iron, will you?

ROY. Ok. (*As Roy moves for the tire iron, Jason enters from R. He's a scrawny adolescent, not athletic, not intellectual. A little nervous, a little mean. He doesn't see Jim under the truck.*)

JASON. Hey, Roy, you seen Jim?

ROY. (*Looking around, unsure of how to respond.*) Jay Bob! Um . . . how come you're asking?

JASON. No reason. Just want to know where he is. I'm thinking of knocking off for the day, you know? (*Jason picks up the tire iron, idly but forcefully hits the truck.*)

ROY. Hey—easy there. You're denting it.

JASON. So what? Fits right in with all the other dents. Go on. Tell me which one's the new one.

ROY. Well . . .

JASON. (*Hitting the truck again.*) It's that one, right there.

ROY. Jay Bob. . . . You really shouldn't . . .

JASON. Why not? (*Hits the truck once more; the radio comes on, playing "T For Texas."\**) Hey neat, the radio came on.

ROY. Jay Bob!!

JASON. Tell Jim I went to invest some of his quarters in the computer industry, ok? (*Hits the truck once more, the radio quits.*) This is a hell of a truck. (*He takes a step left, is suddenly seized by Jim around the ankle.*)

JIM. You should see it from under here.

JASON. (*To Roy.*) Who's under the truck?

JIM. I am, you little thief! Figured my change won't burn, so you're gonna spend it, huh?

JASON. I thought about melting it down . . .

JIM. (*Giving a yank, which topples Jason.*) I'll melt *you* down!

JASON. Help!

*See special note on copyright page.

9

ROY. Jim! Stop it, now!

JIM. (*Dragging him under the truck.*) Were you going to sell my truck, too?! Soon as you stop beating on it?!

JASON. It's not worth selling . . . help!

ROY. (*Grabbing Jason's arms.*) Cut it out, Jim. He's just a kid!

JIM. (*Emerging behind the truck, as he continues to pull Jason.*) You think I should let him live to be an adult!?

ROY. You can't kill him!

JIM. Not if you don't let go, I can't. Jay Bob, did you move those beer cases like I told you?

JASON. No!

JIM. Hear that? He's gotta go, Roy!

ROY. He will! Tomorrow. He'll fly away!

JIM. What if he comes back?

JASON. Why should I come back? I'd rather go to a concentration camp!

JIM. (*Letting go.*) Where's that tire iron? Keep hold of him, Roy.

ROY. Jim, calm down, now . . . (*As Jim picks up the tire iron, Roy lets Jason go. Jason starts to scramble off R.*)

JIM. Damn it!!! (*Jim dives and tackles Jason.*)

JASON. Let go of me!

ROY. Get off him, Jim!

JASON. Let me go, you big turkey!

JIM. (*Slowly raising the tire iron, holding Jason down with his free hand.*) Say goodbye to everything.

ROY. *JIM!!*

JASON. If you hurt me, my Mom'll leave you! (*Jim hesitates.*) She will. You know she will! She'll walk right out and go home to Minnesota. You'll be all alone, you big cracker clown! (*A pause. Jim looks at Jason with disgust, and slowly lowers the tire iron. Jason rises.*) All right. 'Bout time I get a little respect around here.

JIM. Get inside.

JASON. I'll go inside when I want to.

JIM. *Now!!*

JASON. Ok. I want to. (*Jason takes a step for the bar, then suddenly pulls the tire iron out of Jim's hand and strikes the truck once more. The radio comes on, and Jason drops the tire iron and dashes into the bar. Jim roars and starts after him, but Roy gets in his way. The radio plays a Tex-Mex instrumental.*)

ROY. Easy, Jim! Easy! (*A moment of tension. Then Jim suddenly turns and walks determinedly to the back of the truck.*)

JIM. Right.

ROY. That was nice, Jim. You showed nice restraint. (*Jim opens the gate, hops up onto the flatbed.*) What are you doing? (*Jim starts to unfold some canvas that lies in the truck.*) Jim? What are you working on there? Jim? What is that?

JIM. My tent.

ROY. Your what?

JIM. My tent, dammit! If I can't kill that kid, at least I can avoid him. If I can't take my truck someplace else, I can live in it here.

ROY. What are you talking about? You can't—

JIM. Roy. I didn't murder Jay Bob just now. But that don't mean I won't the next time. Safer all around if I stay out here till he's gone. I'll just pretend I'm 200 miles away, that's all.

ROY. You're gonna sleep in your own parking lot?

JIM. It's none of your business, Roy. (*Jim stamps on the flatbed. The radio cuts out.*)

ROY. (*Watching Jim work.*) This is silly . . .

JIM. *I'm doing it! All right?!* Now get on up here and help me.

ROY. Why are you setting it up in the truck?

JIM. Always do. Keeps the snakes away.

ROY. There ain't no snakes on the asphalt here.

JIM. Get in the truck, Roy!

ROY. (*Climbing up.*) Ok, ok.

JIM. Grab that rope there.

ROY. Ok.

11

JIM. And shut up. (*They work.*)

ROY. (*With nervous affability.*) Hey, Jim. ain't this gonna make it hard for you to introduce me to that niece of Eva June's?

JIM. Thought I told you to shut up.

ROY. Well, I think I may love the girl, is all. You know— the way it was with you and Eva June there, in Dallas International. Real sudden-like.

JIM. You're babbling. Hold this.

ROY. (*Holding a tent section.*) No I'm not. Really. I could tell the minute I saw her. Something about her just gave off a special . . . glint, you know?

JIM. Don't drink in the mornings, Roy.

ROY. All the bottles, the 10 High and the Early Times, just glinted. Honest. Hell, even the Old Grandad looked, uh . . . looked sorta . . .

JIM. Younger?

ROY. How old is she, anyway?

JIM. I don't know. About 20 or so.

ROY. Well, I'm only 30.

JIM. Yeah, but you look 45. Come on, pull. (*Roy pulls on a rope.*)

ROY. That's not my fault. I work in the ground. You get pale, working in deep ditches all day.

JIM. Roy, I got other things to think about.

ROY. I know, I know. I just need some information is all. Like, uh . . . like what's her name? You never said.

JIM. Catherine.

ROY. Catherine. That's *pretty*. You ain't gonna fix *her* name, are you?

JIM. Pull on the rope, Roy.

ROY. (*Doing so.*) What else do you know about her?

JIM. Nothing.

ROY. You must know something.

JIM. When Eva June talks about her family, I never listen. I know she's mentioned Catherine a few times, but whatever

12

the hell she said I can't remember.

ROY. Please Jim, anything. Any sort of fact. (*A pause.*)

JIM. There was one thing Eva June said about her, but . . . nah, I can't remember.

ROY. Is she married?

JIM. Did she have a ring on?

ROY. Nope.

JIM. Then I guess she ain't. Turn that flap over.

ROY. We're fated, Jim. I just got that feel, you know? Oh, she may fight it, but it's inevitable. Fate's gonna keep slapping us together until we can't come apart no more.

JIM. One big lump, huh?

ROY. Sorta. And Jim, there's just one thing I'd like to ask you to do.

JIM. What's that?

ROY. Go in there and ask her if she'll go out with me.

JIM. Roy . . .

ROY. You know the bad luck I've had with women. You've seen me in the bar.

JIM. You don't have bad luck.

ROY. I do too. They hit me. They hit me all the time, 'cause I say stupid things. I can't help it, I get nervous, and . . . well, I just don't want to make a bad impression on Catherine. She means too much to me.

JIM. Three seconds is all you saw her.

ROY. I know when I'm in love! (*Jim glares at him.*) Besides, I think she liked me. There was something in her eye.

JIM. Hope she got it out.

ROY. It's time I got serious about a woman.

JIM. You don't want to get serious about a woman.

ROY. Yes I do . . .

JIM. No man in his right mind wants to get serious about a woman.

ROY. You did. (*Jim glares at Roy again.*) You did. Think about that. Wasn't so bad for you.

JIM. What do you think it's like when a woman comes into

your life, anyway? You think it's a big plus or something? You think it's an add-on?

ROY. Well . . . sure.

JIM. Well it ain't! Whenever a woman comes to stay, you're gonna lose something. Never know what it'll be neither. When Eva June came down here the first word outta her mouth was asphalt.

ROY. Asphalt?

JIM. That's right. The parking lot. This asphalt parking lot without any snakes in it. Used to be dirt. Hard-packed dirt, as far as the eye could see — all the way out to the street. This used to be a biker's bar. Did you know that?

ROY. Yeah. This place had a hell of a reputation. I was afraid to come in here.

JIM. (*A bit ruefully.*) You ain't now though, are you?

ROY. Well, anyway, I think asphalt's kind of an improvement.

JIM. You do, do you? I was a biker myself. Had a Harley. Man, that thing just glittered. It was one proud beast, I tell you.

ROY. They can be pretty.

JIM. (*Sarcastically.*) *Pretty?* (*With reverence.*) A Harley stands erect. Like a man, on its own two wheels. Its engine stands erect. Not like the engine in this old swamp . . . (*He strikes the truck: the radio plays a bit of the yodel from "Cowboy's Lullabye"\* before he hits the truck again and the radio cuts out.*) Lying there like some kind of mechanical puddle. Roy, everything about a Harley is poised. You know that?

ROY. (*Nodding.*) Uh-huh.

JIM. No you don't. Don't pretend you do. (*Goes and gets a beer from the cab of the truck.*) Time was, we used to close this bar down, after drinking and fighting and rolling around

\*See special note on copyright page.

in the dirt till dawn, and then we'd just mount up and bust on out for the hills. Up and out. Black knights of the highway. Seeking after a state of pure . . . disconnection. You know?

ROY. Well . . .

JIM. Shut up and blow on this. (*He hands Roy an inflatable pillow. Roy starts to blow it up.*) Those were some kind of weekends, believe me. And it's all changed now. All of it. 'Cause I got serious about a woman. Know what the second thing outta her mouth was?

ROY. What?

JIM. No Harley.

ROY. Really? (*Jim nods.*) So you sold it, huh?

JIM. You don't sell a Harley. I rode it to Utah.

ROY. Utah? Why'd you ride it way out there?

JIM. 'Cause there's a canyon in Utah. And there's a promontory. And there's a river.

ROY. So?

JIM. Were you born thick, or what? I took my bike out to Dead Horse Point, Utah and sailed it off the edge. Ok? It's a mile drop, straight down. At the bottom is the Green River. I sent my Harley out into space over the Green River, and never watched it fall. As far as I'm concerned, it's still going.

ROY. Isn't that dangerous?

JIM. No Roy, *this* is dangerous — trying to have an intelligent conversation with you. (*Pauses.*) Eva June calls motorcycles toys for men. Like that's a bad thing. Like men don't need toys.

ROY. Why don't you leave her?

JIM. You don't know a thing about love.

ROY. Well, I'm trying to find out. Come on, Jim — go inside and talk to Catherine for me, please?

JIM. You really are a glutton for punishment, aren't you? (*Roy nods eagerly.*) Well, I'm not going in.

ROY. Why not?

JIM. Jay Bob's in there, for one thing. I might kill him.

ROY. I'll keep Jay Bob out of your way.

JIM. Pretend I did ask her. And she did go out with you. It's long odds, but let's pretend she did. And let's say for once in your life you didn't say anything stupid, and she actually liked you. What would you do then?

ROY. I'd marry her.

JIM. You'd marry her. But Roy, don't you see what that'd do?

ROY. What?

JIM. Right now you're one of my best customers. You come in every day, you never get loud drunk and you tip too much. It's true you're the dullest man I ever met, but in my bar, that's no real problem. If you married Catherine, though, you'd have the right to take that dullness of yours up outta my bar and into my house. I can't let you do that. (*Pauses.*) Now come on, why don't you go on inside and grab us some sour cream 'n onion chips? I got lots of beer in the truck. We can camp out here in the shade of my tent for awhile. Give us both a chance to cool off. Go on now. There'll be other women. (*Roy starts dejectedly towards the bar, stops.*)

ROY. Sure, you can say that—you already got one. Hell, I know I'm dull. I've always known it. Last time I asked a girl to marry me, she said, "Yes, Ray." I was too embarrassed to correct her. I know I'm dull. You can say you had to sacrifice this and that for Eva June, but my whole life is a sacrifice. I mean, if you're poor, there's always a chance you might get rich. If you're stupid, there's the chance you might get educated, but if you're dull . . .

JIM. I ain't gonna pity you, Roy.

ROY. Well, somebody has to. Some woman has to see me and say to herself, "That man needs help. That man needs the love of a good woman." Why shouldn't it be Catherine? (*Suddenly shouting up to the house.*) Catherine!? Catherine!!

JIM. What the hell are you doing?

ROY. *Hey, Catherine! Hey?! It's me, Roy Manual!*
JIM. Roy!
ROY. *Can I come up and meet you?!*
JIM. Shut up, Roy!
ROY. *Jim won't introduce me, 'cause he thinks I'm boring, but . . . !*
JIM. (*Clapping a hand over Roy's mouth.*) Calm *down*, Roy! (*They listen for a moment.*) I don't think she heard you. (*He relaxes his grip.*)
ROY. *Catherine! You up there!?* (*Jim silences him again.*)
JIM. What are you *doing?* You think this is any way to meet a girl?
ROY. It's the only way I got left.
JIM. Get over in that truck. (*Roy trudges to the truck, sits on the gate.*) You should be ashamed of yourself. Shouting at a woman you never met. You think she's a cocker spaniel, that comes when you call?
ROY. I'm sorry, I just . . .
JIM. You just nothing. This is not the jungle, Roy Manual. This is Houston, Texas.
ROY. I know . . .
JIM. This is an asphalt parking lot I'm standing on.
ROY. Sorry. (*A pause.*)
JIM. Now you behave. And *maybe* later I'll introduce you to her, like a human being. All right?
ROY. Would you? Oh, thanks, Jim. I knew you'd . . .
JIM. Shut up.
ROY. All right.
JIM. Not that she'd have anything to do with you anyway. (*Going to get two beers in the cab of truck.*) I mean, what's an educated northern girl gonna want with a laid-off ditch digger from Houston?
ROY. I ain't laid off. I'm on accidental sick leave. Hell, cave-ins happen all the time. I go back next week. Got nearly all my memory back.

JIM. Let me rephrase the question: what's an educated northern girl gonna want with a wrecked-up ditch digger from Houston?

ROY. (*As they sit on the gate of the truck and drink.*) You think I got nothing to offer, don't you? You think I'm satisfied to burrow in the ground my whole life. Well I ain't. I'm fixing to move up. Know what I did this week?

JIM. What?

ROY. Enrolled myself in a college.

JIM. College? You don't even have a high-school . . .

ROY. Don't need one. I enrolled in a two-year bachelor's certification program at the College of the Floodplain, down in Bonne Aire, Texas. They don't require a high school diploma to get in. Just grit.

JIM. Sounds like a hell of a school.

ROY. It's a start. And there's no telling how far you can go, if you stick with it.

JIM. (*Nods, unconvinced.*) Uh-huh.

ROY. Well, it's true. Hell, anybody can go to college if they want to bad enough. Here, look at this. (*He takes an old, worn newspaper clipping out of his wallet.*)

JIM. What's that?

ROY. It's a story I read in the paper a few years ago. Kept it with me for inspiration. It's all about how some students at Harvard University worked it out how to enroll a pig.

JIM. A pig?

ROY. That's right. They just gave him a name, and some good test scores, and sneaked all that into some computer someplace — and before you knew it, that pig was a freshman at Harvard.

JIM. He must've seemed kinda noticeable in class.

ROY. Nope, not really. See, they did it all on paper somehow — just sent in grades at the end of the semester or something. I'm not sure how they did it — it's in there, though.

JIM. A pig, huh?

ROY. They got him through a whole four-year program, too. He even got a degree.
JIM. What in?
ROY. Humanities. One of the other students even made a commencement speech, and called him the most well-rounded graduate in Harvard history.
JIM. What's all this supposed to mean, Roy?
ROY. Well, like I say—it's been an inspiration. I mean, if a pig can do that well at Harvard, I oughta clean up down in Bonne Aire.
JIM. I'm not introducing you to Catherine, Roy.
ROY. You just said you would . . .
JIM. I don't think you're really ready for a woman.
ROY. I am too. Come on now, you promised. Take me up there right now.
JIM. No.
ROY. Come on—I been nice. I sat here drinking beer and philosophizing with you, and now I need a woman. It's time for love.
JIM. Love, huh?
ROY. Yeah. Love.
JIM. (*Sighs.*) Roy, you don't know what you're messing with here. Love. You may as well say you're ready for a hurricane or an epidemic or a flood. Love don't repair your life, it wrecks it.
ROY. How do you mean?
JIM. Look, say your life's a tv show, ok? Something you can grasp.
ROY. Ok. What show?
JIM. I don't know—*CHiPS* or something. Where the cops ride around on their bikes all day, saving people so they can go to bed with 'em later?
ROY. Yeah . . . ?
JIM. Well, now, let's say one of those cops gets married. Suddenly, he won't be riding around saving and bed-hopping in quite the same way, will he? 'Cause now he's got

a serious woman at home, who'll seriously kill him if he tries it, right?

ROY. Well . . .

JIM. So suddenly we're talking a whole new tv show, ain't we? Something more like *Hart To Hart* or *Ironsides* or something, you see? Something with limitations.

ROY. Yeah . . .

JIM. I'm not saying you don't still have a good program, but somewhere in there you changed channels without even realizing it. You see what I mean?

ROY. I guess.

JIM. It's the chance you take when you fool around with a proven formula.

ROY. But you took a chance—with Eva June.

JIM. And I got a whole new tv show, didn't I? Called *Leave It To Jay Bob*. The ratings are lousy, believe you me. And I'm looking forward to a life full of reruns. (*Pauses.*) And that's only part of it. Being with Eva June hasn't just stopped me from being a biker, you know. It's stopped me from being the meanest, baddest, cruelest, dirtiest, toughest, most vicious . . . and happiest biker of 'em all. Hell, I could out-drink, out-fight, out-think and out-hump anybody in town. And I got plenty of practice, too. Every once in awhile one of the other boys'd slow up, get married. I watched 'em do it. And I thanked my damn stars that a fate such as that could never come to a man as dangerous and disgusting as me. Then I met Eva June on the day I turned 40. (*Long pause.*) She ain't the most beautiful woman I ever met. She ain't even the smartest, in some ways. And she ain't the nicest, either. And hell—she's not even in love with me. Says she never will be. But I took one look, and I knew I'd never be rid of her. (*Slight pause, quietly.*) And look where it's gotten me. Me. The most fearsome man in southwest Houston. Without my bike. Sitting in a damn truck that I can't even make go. (*A beat, with disgust.*) You want to know the worst part? I'm satisfied. (*Pauses.*) See what I mean? Suddenly you're on a

20

whole new tv show. Suddenly you're on . . . *You Asked For It*, or *My Mother The Truck* or something, I don't know.

ROY. (*Quietly.*) Well, Jim . . . I guess that all may be true. And I'm sorry for you if it is. But I'm a man who wants to change channels. Hell, I feel like I had the *Farm Report* on all my life. I want to see some prime time. I'm going in there.

JIM. (*As Roy starts for the house.*) Hold on, Roy . . .

ROY. Thanks for the beer.

JIM. (*Grabbing him.*) You ain't going in there.

ROY. I want a new show!

JIM. It's too dangerous. What if you get *Flipper* or something?

ROY. (*Tearing away.*) I *don't* care! (*He tries for the door, but Jim blocks his path. So he rushes for the truck and honks the horn instead.*) Catherine! Catherine honey!?

JIM. (*Going for him.*) Damn you . . . !

ROY. *Come on down and meet the pride of Texas!* (*Jim whirls Roy away from the horn.*)

JIM. Damn it, Roy — shut up!

ROY. No!

JIM. Go home. Will you? Will you just go home?

ROY. No! I got a right to meet her!

JIM. You ain't got a right to nothing!! Get outta here, right now!

ROY. No! I'm in love! And damn you to hell for getting in my way, you big son of a . . .

JIM. (*Pulling back his fist to hit him, then pausing, staring at him.*) Don't you hate love? Don't you just *hate* it?

ROY. What?

JIM. Look at us. Look what love did to us. We used to be friends, sort of. And now. . . . It's just pitiful.

ROY. (*A bit ashamed.*) I don't know what you're talking about.

JIM. Just pitiful. (*Jason enters from the bar.*)

JASON. What's all the yelling about?

JIM. I thought I told you to stay inside.

JASON. Who's doing all the yelling and the honking? Catherine came down; she thought someone's yelling at her.

ROY. I was. Is she in the bar?

JASON. What were you yelling at her for?

ROY. (*Dashing into the bar.*) I love her, that's why.

JIM. *Roy!*

JASON. (*As Jim starts after Roy.*) He loves her? That's pretty funny.

JIM. (*Stops.*) What's funny about it?

JASON. Huh? Nothing. Just that . . .

JIM. There's nothing funny about a man's love. Even Roy's. Love's the biggest thing you give up in your whole damn life. Remember that.

JASON. Ok. Just think it's funny that he loves Catherine, that's all.

JIM. Why shouldn't he love her? Give me one good reason why he shouldn't love that woman.

JASON. She's a nun.

JIM. (*Pausing a moment, wincing as he remembers.*) *That's* the thing I couldn't remember about her! She's a nun! Oh, why don't I listen to Eva June better? How come Catherine's not wearing nun clothes?

JASON. I don't know. Think her order gave it up or something.

JIM. She's a nun. *Damn!* Roy's gonna hate to hear that.

JASON. Yeah. Funny, ain't it?

JIM. Shut up. We ain't gonna tell him.

JASON. He's probably finding out from her right now.

ROY. (*Returning.*) Dammit. Oh, damn it.

JIM. What's wrong, Roy? Disappointment?

ROY. She wasn't there. Must've gone upstairs again.

JASON. (*Snickers.*) That's too bad.

JIM. Shut up, Jay Bob.

ROY. I was gonna ask her out, too.

JASON. (*The snicker becomes a laugh.*) Good idea, Roy.

JIM. (*To Jason.*) You get in the bar! Now! Get the hell *in* there!

JASON. (*Exiting.*) Don't give up, Roy!

JIM. *Now!!* (*Jason exits into the bar, laughing.*) I'm coming in there in a minute, and you better be working! I'm gonna be on your butt all day, you vicious little creep! (*Jim hops up on the truck, begins to take down the tent.*)

ROY. Well, I came close, anyhow. Almost saw her.

JIM. Yeah, Roy. You . . . came close.

ROY. What are you doing now?

JIM. Taking it down.

ROY. You just got it up.

JIM. Don't need it. I'm gonna ride that kid into the ground in what little time he's got here. He's gonna wish he'd never set foot in my bar.

ROY. Aren't you afraid of killing him?

JIM. What I got in mind is worse. Little turd, laughing at you like that.

ROY. Everybody laughs at me.

JIM. (*Stops, stares at Roy.*) Well, they shouldn't. (*He resumes taking the tent down.*)

ROY. Say, Jim?

JIM. What?

ROY. You think I'll ever meet Catherine?

JIM. Um . . . sure. 'Course you will. I'll introduce you myself, um . . . soon as I . . . soon as I work myself up to it.

ROY. Ok.

JIM. Let's get drunk first.

ROY. (*Smiling.*) Not too drunk.

JIM. (*Going to cab for beers.*) You want some music?

ROY. Sure.

JIM. (*Receiving a shock from the radio.*) Aaaagh! *Damn!* Forget the music. (*He hands Roy a beer.*)

ROY. Thanks. Hell, this is the most we drunk together since I've known you, ain't it?

JIM. (*As they sit on the gate.*) Yes, it is.

ROY. I know she'll like me—when we finally do meet. I could tell, even in those three little seconds.

JIM. You never know, Roy. Maybe she's got . . . things wrong with her.

ROY. (*Disbelievingly.*) Like what?

JIM. Well . . . Jay Bob just told me that she's, um . . . Catholic.

ROY. (*Disappointed.*) Shoot. (*Bucking up again.*) Well, so what? She's pretty.

JIM. No good being pretty if you got to go to confession all the time.

ROY. If I married her, she wouldn't have nothing to confess. (*A pause. Jim looks him up and down.*)

JIM. Well, maybe you got a point there, Roy.

ROY. (*Smiles.*) It's great being in love, ain't it?

JIM. Yeah . . . just great. (*The radio comes on suddenly, playing Elvis Presley's "Wise Men Say."\* Jim looks around at it, annoyed, and strikes the truck. The song continues. Jim strikes the truck again. The song continues. Jim sighs, shakes his head, takes a swig of beer and stares into the distance as lights fade and the music plays on.*)

*See special note on copyright page.

# ACT TWO

*The scene is an outdoor deck, on the third floor of
an old house, the bottom floor of which is a bar.
Behind the deck is the peaked roof of the house, and
a small door, converted from an attic window. A
street light is visible Stage Right, and the top of a
telephone pole is Stage Left. On the deck, which is
surrounded by a simple railing, are a couple cheap
but comfortable pieces of furniture — chaise, chair,
etc. Also a sizeable flower pot, with soil but no
flower, and a hibachi. Just below the deck, is the
back of a sign which runs down the building out of
sight.*

*Catherine Empanger is on the deck. She's dressed
very simply in dark, casual clothes. She sits on the
chaise reading. She closes the book, looks around
restlessly. She stands, slowly moves into an
amateurish try at a two-step while singing quietly to
herself.*

CATHERINE. The skies at night . . . are big and bright —
deep in the heart of Tex-as . . . (*We suddenly hear Hank
Williams singing, "Your Cheatin' Heart."* She turns, walks

*See special note on copyright page.

25

*U. and looks down over the railing. Over the song offstage a male voice shouts from below.*)

VOICE. (*Off.*) Now that is music! Ain't it? That is no damn shit. (*Another voice laughs derisively.*) That's none of your mulepuke Kenny Rogers muppet show horse crap! That is Hank Williams—the King of music! (*A moment passes, as Catherine listens. She starts to sway to the music, a little awkwardly. Eve enters from the house. She's wearing a cowboy shirt, jeans and loafers. She carries a hammer and nails. She is smiling, robust. and speaks in a broad Texas accent.*)

EVE. There you are. There you are. We got you treed, don't we? I'm sorry, honey. Didn't mean to drive you way up here. That's what happened, isn't? You were looking for a quiet place in this madhouse and you just kept on rising till you found one. (*Looking over the railing.*) Not too quiet even up here. That juke box sure carries, don't it? Well, hold on—I got a little project to take care of, then we'll get that door shut and it'll be quiet as you please. (*Shouting down.*) Hey! Hey, down there! I'm shouting!

CATHERINE. Eve, you don't have to . . .

EVE. Don't worry. They always hear me eventually. (*Shouting.*) Come on you boys! I'm shouting up here! Jim! Roy! T.R.!

ROY'S VOICE. (*Off.*) Who's that?

EVE. Up here, Roy! Look up! That's right!

ROY. (*Off.*) Oh, howdy, Eva June!

EVE. Do me a favor, Roy—toss up that rock down there. The one with the rope around it?

ROY. (*Off.*) What? Oh, sure! Here goes!

EVE. Watch out, Honey. (*A rock with a line tied to it lands on the roof.*) Thanks, Roy. Now could you shut that door down there? My little niece and me are drowning in Hánk Williams.

ROY. (*Off.*) Your niece up there with you? Let me say hello to her and I'll shut the door.

EVE. Come on now, Roy . . .

ROY. (*Off.*) Just want to say hi.

EVE. (*To Catherine.*) Want to say hello to that Roy fella, honey? You saw him in the bar this morning, I think. (*Catherine pauses, goes to the railing.*)

ROY. (*Off.*) Evening, Miss Empanger! (*Catherine waves, almost imperceptibly.*) Will you be coming down later? I'd like you to dance with me is all.

CATHERINE. I don't know . . .

ROY. (*Off.*) What? You'd *like* to dance with me?

CATHERINE. (*Louder.*) I don't know.

EVE. Shut that door, Roy, or I'll come down there and dance *on* you! (*The door closes, cutting off the music.*) There. That's better. Almost livable out here now, ain't it? Imagine that Roy Manual holding us hostage that way just to get a dance with you. (*Starting to pull up the rope attached to the rock.*) The men in this bar sure take some getting used to. I got half a mind to tell him all about you. That'd shut him up.

CATHERINE. No—I'd rather you didn't.

EVE. Why not? Nothing's wrong with being a nun.

CATHERINE. I'm not a nun, though. I'm . . .

EVE. Nothing wrong with being a novice, then. Hell, I'm not ashamed of you. You should let me tell Roy. He'd leave you alone for sure.

CATHERINE. No. People . . . get nervous when they hear that about me. Jim, for instance.

EVE. Jim just hates Catholics, that's all. (*Stops pulling.*) He's treated you all right today, hasn't he?

CATHERINE. Oh, sure—pretty much. Once this afternoon he sort of . . . came up and stared at me.

EVE. Did he say anything?

CATHERINE. He just said, "A nun," shook his head and went back down. I haven't seen him since. I've been up here all day. Trying not to be any trouble.

EVE. How could you be any trouble?

CATHERINE. (*As Eve begins pulling again.*) Showing up

unannounced, for one thing. I'm sure you weren't too happy about that. What is that you're doing?

EVE. Pulling up a banner for the Labor Day weekend. Says, "Work Hard Drink Hard". Made it myself. Brings in business. (*Starting to nail it to the rail.*) I'll tell you something, honey. You got an open invitation here. Couldn't be any trouble if you tried. It's so good to see my sister's little girl again. When I got your call last night, I was dancing around in a little circle, I was so happy. So talk to me — how's your life going?

CATHERINE. Oh . . . fine. (*She moves away, kneels down by the hibachi.*) Do you use this much?

EVE. That? not since last spring. Too hot out here in the summer. You're lucky it's September. Houston in July is inhuman. (*Finishing the banner.*) There.

CATHERINE. It looks a little grimy.

EVE. What? Houston?

CATHERINE. No — the grill.

EVE. There's probably birds nesting in it, for all I know. Why are you . . . ?

CATHERINE. I thought I could cook something.

EVE. Cook? Honey, I'm taking you out for dinner. Sweet Jesus, you think you got to do for yourself up here on the roof?

CATHERINE. I was only . . .

EVE. I'm taking you somewhere nice. We'll leave in about a half-hour, ok?

CATHERINE. Ok.

EVE. (*Smiling.*) Eating alone. Hell, I thought it was your mother that was mad at me, not you.

CATHERINE. Oh, I'm not mad at you. Really, I'm not. And Mom isn't either, really. Not really.

EVE. Sure. That's why I haven't heard from her in six months, huh? (*Pause.*) Well, I don't blame her. It's a hard thing for her to accept. One minute I seem to be a happily married mother of one, the next minute I'm divorced, leav-

ing my kid behind, and trotting down to southeast Texas with some shitkicker I met in an airport. That was a lot to throw her way all at once. Especially when I keep telling her it's all for the best. (*Pauses.*) It is, though. I'm a new person. Hell, I'm not a *new* person, I'm a person at all. That's the difference. It's like where I was all day today. Going to business meetings. *Business* meetings. Me. How about that? Never happened when I was with Robert.
CATHERINE. But Robert was your husband. You had a marriage with Robert.
EVE. I had something with him, all right. Maybe that was marriage, who knows? (*A pause. Eve shudders.*) Robert. I can't believe it sometimes when I think of the things he used to make me do.
CATHERINE. Uncle Robert? (*As Eve nods solemnly.*) What things?
EVE. Deadly things.
CATHERINE. Uncle *Robert*?
EVE. Honey, your "uncle Robert" is a deadly human being. Deadly dull.
CATHERINE. (*Sighing with relief, then reproachfully.*) Eve! You had me really scared there for a minute.
EVE. You should have been. Honey, Robert is a terminally boring man. That's nothing to laugh about. In fact, he's the most boring man possible: he's a professor of Latvian.
CATHERINE. Well, I know, but . . .
EVE. And when you're a professor of Latvian, there's only eight other people in the whole world who care. I discovered I wasn't one of 'em, and I knew I was in trouble right then. 'Cause he kept trying to make me one, kept demanding that I care who the kings—or whatever they were—of ancient Lativa were. And the more I said, "No baby, I am not interested to learn about the Hanseatic League," the angrier he'd get. And you know, the angrier he got the cooler and more logical he'd be. That's when it really got dangerous. 'Cause then he'd prove to me, literally prove, beyond the

shadow of a doubt, that I could not go through another day without becoming a dedicated scholar of Baltic Studies. So, after a few hours of listening to him, I would numbly nod my head, pick up some learned paper by a colleague of his — one of the eight — and study it like a little schoolgirl with her homework assignment before bed. And he would just sit there beaming at me. The next morning I always woke up knowing the coordinates of Riga and wondering how to kill my husband. (*Pauses.*) Well I knew that wasn't a healthy situation. And about that time I met Jim, while changing planes — the luckiest connection of my life — and he took one look at me and knew just what to say.

CATHERINE. What was that?

EVE. He said, "I got a bar in Houston. Interested?" I was. Well, look at that.

CATHERINE. What?

EVE. That shingle's falling off. I might as well fix that right now. You don't mind, do you?

CATHERINE. Um . . . no . . .

EVE. (*Straightening it.*) I mean, the next thing you know, there's water damage. I just love going around this place with a hammer and nails. Always something to fix. (*She starts to pound.*)

CATHERINE. Eve, maybe I better just go.

EVE. Go? What are you talking about? You just got here.

CATHERINE. I know, but . . . you're so busy, and . . . I do have a standing invitation at Aunt Margaret's . . .

EVE. (*Intercepting her.*) Don't be silly . . .

CATHERINE. I'm not. I just don't feel like I'm . . . fitting in here. I mean, this is a bar, and I come from a convent, and you're not married to the man you live with, and men keep shouting at me, and . . . Aunt Margaret would just be . . .

EVE. Aunt Margaret hasn't taken a deep breath in 25 years.

CATHERINE. Well, then . . . maybe Aunt Camilla . . .

EVE. Aunt Camilla is fat. And she hates men. And she hates

women, too. Why on earth would you want to go see Aunt Camilla? (*Catherine pauses.*) Face it, honey. I'm the only relative you got that knows how to listen with both ears. Now you sit down while I finish pounding this sucker. (*Catherine hesitates, sits down. Eve pounds.*)

CATHERINE. At least my other aunts didn't walk out on their husband and son.

EVE. What?

CATHERINE. At least . . .

EVE. I heard you. Honey, when I walked out, it was not only for me. It was for Robert too. *And* for little Jay Bob.

CATHERINE. Jay Bob? You mean Jason?

EVE. That's right.

CATHERINE. *Jay Bob?*

EVE. Ain't it cute? That's what we call him now, while he's visiting. Jay Bob. Names just naturally get changed in Texas. Hell, I'm Eva June to most of these folks. Eva June Wilfong. Whoo! (*Pauses, admires her work on the shingle.*) There now. Let it rain. I'll tell you a little secret, Catherine: Jay Bob's better off since I moved down here. You know why?

CATHERINE. Why?

EVE. 'Cause now he's got a real mother to deal with in me. Now he's got an honest-to-God human being, 'stead of just a dead hum coming out of someone else's machine. (*A beat.*) It's been a real kick in the butt having him down here this summer. 'Course, he and Jim get into a fight now and then, but that's only natural.

CATHERINE. How often do they fight?

EVE. Every day. But no broken bones yet. (*Smiles suddenly.*) Oh, how do you like my new accent? I forgot you never heard it before this morning.

CATHERINE. Well, it's, um . . . it's . . .

EVE. It's a dinger, ain't it? I was only here a couple months before I was talking more Texas than the Texans. Well, why not? I get along better with folks this way. Besides, Jim and

31

I think it's good for business.

CATHERINE. Are you and Jim ever . . . going to get married?

EVE. Why should we?

CATHERINE. Well, you live together, and . . .

EVE. That's right. Living together is for having someone around. Marriage is for having someone around your neck. Jim and me share what we can about each other, and leave the rest alone. We don't mess around on the side, and we don't worry about love. 'Least, I don't.

CATHERINE. But love is . . .

EVE. Love is an evil pain in the butt. For years, I was in love with a man who had more passion for Latvian self-rule than he had for my body. You can stick love. Besides, the real treat for me down here is this place. This little tavern is just heaven for me.

CATHERINE. Why? I mean . . .

EVE. That's all right. I know it looks strange, but this here bar is one place I can *affect*. Look at that railing!

CATHERINE. What?

EVE. It's practically falling apart. I'm glad I came up. (*She straddles the railing, starts to pound.*) Maintainance — that's what keeps a business alive. (*The bar door opens. We hear a bit of "Red-Neck Mother" by Jerry Jeff Walker\* before it closes. Eve calls down.*) Hey, Joe Bill! Hey, Larry Lee! How's it going? (*We hear voices calling up.*)

VOICE. Hey, Eva June!

2ND VOICE. Don't fall off, now!

EVE. I won't! Boy, this place sure has changed. You should've seen it when I got here. I near puked. Really. There was a broken-down sign that said, "JIM STOOLS BAR;" there was beer and broken glass on the floor; there was bikers coming in every night swearing, fighting, committing crimes of all kinds. Well, I told Jim he'd got me there all right, but

\*See special note on copyright page.

if he wanted to keep me, things were going to change. So he just backed off and let me go at it. It's only been one year, but come here and look at this parking lot. (*Catherine approaches, looks down.*) Asphalt. Not dirt like there was. Not one damn motorcycle, either. Pickup trucks. Solid, dependable pickup trucks. This is a workingman's bar now. (*Taking Catherine towards the door.*) And look at this. (*Turning on the lights for the sign.*) A new name. With a message. "NICE PEOPLE DANCING TO GOOD COUNTRY MUSIC BAR." My idea. Honey, if you call yourself nice people, nice people'll come. If you call yourself dancing, then they'll dance, instead of spreading their fat, leather-covered rears on a barstool and letting farts all night. And if you play *good* country music, well, folks'll be elevated, 'stead of teased and titillated. There's a hall-of-fame juke-box down there now. Same way on weekends, too. Dance bands. For nice people. And Jim loves it. Wasn't sure he would, but he does.
CATHERINE. Well, it's . . . it's a very nice bar.
EVE. We're going to make it a restaurant.
CATHERINE. Really?
EVE. (*Nodding, quivering with pleasure.*) That's where I was all day, after I got you at the airport. Non-stop meetings with the contractors. In six months this is going to be the "NICE PEOPLE EATING TO GOOD COUNTRY MUSIC RESTAURANT." People'll pop in here like salmon up a ladder. God, I'm happy! (*Pauses.*) How're you doing? I been talking all evening. What'd you do all day while I was gone?
CATHERINE. Well, I was . . . um, reading . . . up here. (*Eve picks up the book from the chaise.*)
EVE. *Sexual Advice For Teens.* Kind of a strange selection.
CATHERINE. Oh, I just . . . found it downstairs.
EVE. I got it for Jay Bob. It's kind of advanced—says sex is ok, and like that. Why were you reading it? I thought you were getting all ready to be nunnified.
CATHERINE. Well, nuns have to deal with sex. You know—advising, and . . .

33

EVE. Advising against, as I recall. So how long 'til you get to be a nun, anyway? You going to be a novice all your life?

CATHERINE. Well, I've . . . been on retreat for awhile . . .

EVE. Retreat? How do you retreat from a convent? Sounds redundant.

CATHERINE. It's possible.

EVE. Just shows my ignorance. But you know me. Not the world's best Catholic. Fact, I'm a Methodist, now—that's how bad a Catholic I've become. (*Catherine looks at her with surprise.*) I didn't tell you about that, did I?

CATHERINE. No.

EVE. Well, I got tired of confession, but I still liked organ music. So, why were you on retreat?

CATHERINE. (*Moving towards the hibachi.*) You know, I really could cook up here . . .

EVE. You dodging the question?

CATHERINE. No. I like eating simply.

EVE. It's no shame to go on retreat, is it?

CATHERINE. No, it's just . . . no, it isn't.

EVE. (*Jokingly.*) I mean, it's not like them kicking you out or something. (*Pause.*) Is it?

CATHERINE. They don't kick people out. That's not how they do it.

EVE. How do they do it?

CATHERINE. They ask them to go on retreat.

EVE. (*Quietly.*) I see.

CATHERINE. And if that doesn't work out, they ask you if you wouldn't be more comfortable in a secular mode.

EVE. Secular mode? That sounds like IBM. Oh, honey, I had no idea . . . (*She goes to hug Catherine, who moves away.*)

CATHERINE. No. I mean, I'm not unhappy. There's no need. Really.

EVE. But you always wanted to be a nun. When you were nine years old, you used to talk about it. Oh, honey. What happened? Why'd they . . . ?

CATHERINE. It was just the logical outcome of . . . certain events, that's all.

EVE. What events?

CATHERINE. Things I said. (*The bar door opens downstairs. For a moment we hear Johnny Cash singing, "I fell in to a burning ring of fire . . ."* then silence again.)

EVE. What things did you say?

CATHERINE. Not bad things. Nothing awful, really. Just inappropriate things. Things that made people in a strict order uncomfortable.

EVE. Political things?

CATHERINE. Oh, no. No.

EVE. Reform kinds of things?

CATHERINE. No, not reform. Dirty words.

EVE. Dirty words? (*The bar door opens again. We hear, "I fell down, down, down and the flames they got higher . . ."* before it closes again.)

CATHERINE. It's a very sort of unexpected but not entirely unheard-of syndrome I developed recently.

EVE. Dirty words, huh?

CATHERINE. I noticed it one day a few months ago. I was going to breakfast one morning—a morning like any other morning—and I passed one of the sisters in the hallway. She's a woman I saw every day, someone I'd never harbored an evil thought about. She smiled as she went by, looking serene, and I smiled back at her and said, "Isn't this a lovely morning, Sister Shit?". (*Eve laughs despite herself, covers her mouth.*) I don't know where it came from. It's one of my clearest memories, though: the look on her face, the way she recovered almost at once, and asked me to excuse her, but she hadn't quite heard . . . And even *I* wasn't sure at that moment, just what I'd said. I couldn't have said what I thought I'd . . . So anyway, I smiled pleasantly and apologetically,

*See special note on copyright page.

and took a deep breath, and said, "You heard me, Fart-face," and walked on.

EVE. You didn't.

CATHERINE. I did.

EVE. Well, I'll be damned. I always wanted to say that to a nun.

CATHERINE. I swear I didn't mean to. Sister Beatrice never hurt me in her life. She was one of the ones I liked best. And it't not even a matter of that. We're in the same holy order, we're children of God.

EVE. You never heard a kid swear?

CATHERINE. Don't tease me.

EVE. I'm sorry. Why'd you do it?

CATHERINE. I had to. It just came out of me. Like speaking in tongues or something. The words just leaped out of me. They had to be spoken. That's what my psychologist said.

EVE. You saw a psychologist?

CATHERINE. Wouldn't you? I saw everybody. I saw lots of people in the Church: priests, nuns, bishops—everyone.

EVE. How'd that go?

CATHERINE. I cussed them out. All of them. Except God and my psychologist. Eve, I never meant to say any of those things. But I couldn't help it. I started swearing like a linebacker every time I saw the convent. And I'd say other things, too.

EVE. Like what?

CATHERINE. Irrational things. I'd recite the backs of Wheaties boxes. Not at breakfast—other times: during devotions, working in the garden. I didn't even know I read the backs of *Wheaties* boxes. It was just there, suddenly, word for word.

EVE. Why Wheaties?

CATHERINE. I don't know, it's what we ate. But other things, too. Things I'd heard on the radio, rules from games

I played as a kid, bird calls, sounds from comic books: Bam! Rat-a-tat-tat! Ka-boom! Usually during meditation.

EVE. What did the psychologist think?

CATHERINE. That I wasn't cut out to be a nun. He said I was unconsciously trying to break out of the constraints of convent life.

EVE. He sure you don't just like dirty words?

CATHERINE. It's not the obscenity. I got no bigger thrill saying fart-face than yelling "red light green light" or barking like a dog. It was the impropriety of it. That's all I wanted. To shock people. To shock myself.

EVE. Guess it worked, huh?

CATHERINE. I've been numb for months. I mean, there I was—I had everything planned out. I was committed to a life of service in the Church, and suddenly it was . . . Sister Shit.

EVE. What did your folks say?

CATHERINE. Nothing helpful. I went home to explain— you know, maybe stay a week? I was there three days. They couldn't believe I'd failed at 'my life's mission.' They spent the whole time whimpering like a pair of lost puppies. (*Sighs.*) Finally, Mom accused me of wanting to have children, and I left.

EVE. And you came down here?

CATHERINE. I didn't know where to go. Nobody up there would talk to me. And I didn't want to go see Aunt Margaret.

EVE. Well, I am glad you came to see me. What do you think you'll do now? In life, I mean.

CATHERINE. Live a normal life, I guess. I always thought I'd be special, a little more . . . something than the usual person. But I'm just the usual person.

EVE. Don't feel sorry for yourself. Hell, people, don't end up what they plan to be. Except awful people. I planned to be a brain-dead housewife by now; am I?

CATHERINE. Not quite.

EVE. Stick with me, Kid. You'll become one extraordinary usual person. Why were you reading this book? (*i.e., Sexual Advice For Teens.*)

CATHERINE. What? Oh . . . well . . . no reason.

EVE. Honey, I got a whole library down there, and this is the only book that deals with . . .

CATHERINE. I was concerned about . . . mating.

EVE. Mating?

CATHERINE. Yes. Um, mating. You know, men and women and . . .

EVE. I know what it is. Why are you concerned about that?

CATHERINE. Why shouldn't I be?

EVE. No reason. Just seems like we're getting out of the convent awful fast here. How soon you fixing to mate?

CATHERINE. Not soon. It's not the physical aspects I'm worried about—I know all that . . .

EVE. You do, huh?

CATHERINE. But being around men and . . . dating. It's just that I always assumed I'd be a nun. I didn't think about boys. Now, I'll naturally begin to encounter them more. And—well, I couldn't exactly bring it up with Mom.

EVE. Bring it up with me, then. What do you want to know?

CATHERINE. Oh . . . I can read the book.

EVE. Not as good as a live witness. You still a virgin?

CATHERINE. Eve!

EVE. Well, you're a nun—figured you *might* be.

CATHERINE. What I mean is, I can't answer that.

EVE. Why not? Am I asking in Spanish?

CATHERINE. It's just a very private thing.

EVE. Kind of hard to get a read on you, if I don't know what your experience is.

CATHERINE. Nil. It's nil. I don't know a thing. Ok? Just start anywhere.

EVE. Ok. Let's see: men. Men are . . . not like you and me.

CATHERINE. You can go faster than that.

EVE. I better not. Men have different goals, mostly. And

ROY. (*Off.*) Howdy, Catherine! Listen to this! (*He opens the bar door. We hear Hall singing "And I-I-I love you, too."* *He closes the door.*) How about that? Ready to dance now? I'm getting pretty determined down here.

EVE. You're getting pretty well-oiled, is what you're getting.

CATHERINE. Um . . . well, maybe later.

ROY. (*Off.*) What's wrong with right now? Come on down and take a twirl!

CATHERINE. Well . . .

ROY. Come on, baby!

EVE. Roy Manual, do you know who you are asking up here to "take a twirl"? A nun.

ROY. (*Off.*) What?

CATHERINE. Eve . . .

EVE. That's right! My niece is a nun. You are coming on to a bride of Christ.

*See special note on copyright page.

ROY. (*Off.*) I don't care if she's the Bride of Frankenstein, send her down!

EVE. Roy! I can't believe you said that.

ROY. (*Off.*) Well, you don't really expect me to believe that she's a . . . that she's a . . . (*Pause.*) She's a nun?

EVE. She damn sure is. Didn't Jim tell you? (*To Catherine.*) I suppose Jim wouldn't — he hates talking to Roy.

CATHERINE. Roy, I'm not a nun. I'm a novice.

ROY. (*Off.*) A what?

EVE. (*To Catherine.*) Quiet.

CATHERINE. (*To Eve.*) Well, you're not being accurate. I was never a nun.

EVE. Accuracy ain't the point. You want to dance with him?

CATHERINE. Well, I don't know.

ROY. (*Off.*) Hey! Are you a nun or not? What's the verdict?

EVE. She's a nun, Roy! She's a mother superior!

*See special note on copyright page.

39

one of those goals is to keep as much to themselves as possible. That's why they're always turning up in other parts of town with other women, or working 75 hours a week, or ignoring you to watch tv till they can't even answer the simplest questions.

CATHERINE. Or reading Latvian?

EVE. (*Smiling.*) And when they aren't sitting all day like a stone idol, they're heading over the hills to do whatever doesn't include you. This they call freedom, but what it really is, is them just being afraid to get to know us. Takes a man about fifteen hundred years to get to know a woman. In the meantime, all we're left with is the hills. It's like the Bible says: "The hills abideth; and the men just get lost."

CATHERINE. Well . . . what hope is there in that?

EVE. Not much. A little, though. Sometimes you find a man who's capable of improvement. Jim is. He's coming along slow, but he's coming. But I'll give you a tip: it's a good precaution to learn how to love the hills, 'cause you're going to see a lot more of them than you will of most men. That's what Houston's all about for me.

CATHERINE. I don't see many hills here.

EVE. We're standing on one. The NICE PEOPLE DANCING TO GOOD COUNTRY MUSIC BAR. (*The bar door opens. We hear Tom T. Hall singing, "I Love."* Roy calls from below.*)

ROY. (*Off.*) Hey! Hey, up there! Eva June!? You around?!

EVE. (*Going to the railing.*) Dear God. What is it, Roy? Can't you leave us in . . . ?

ROY. (*Off.*) Let me talk to that niece of yours again!

EVE. No, I'm not going to let you talk to . . .

ROY. (*Off.*) Please? I got to say something to her right now! (*Pause.*) You want me to come up there? I will!

EVE. Honey? It's better'n him coming up.

CATHERINE. (*Moving to the rail.*) Yes, Roy?

*See special note on copyright page.

CATHERINE. (*Suddenly calling down.*) No, I'm not! Uh—
I'm not a nun, Roy. I used to be a novice, but I'm not even
that anymore. I'm nothing. (*With an uncertain look at Eve.*)
And I'd be proud to dance with you.
ROY. (*Off.*) You would? Great!
EVE. Are you crazy? What are you doing?
CATHERINE. I'm dancing with Roy Manual.
ROY. (*Off.*) You want to come down?
EVE. (*To Catherine.*) Why?!
CATHERINE. Well, why not? I've got to get started
sometime.
EVE. But . . . dinner.
CATHERINE. Just one dance.
ROY. (*Off.*) Or would you rather I came up?
EVE. Down, Roy! You stay down! Honey, let me talk to you
first . . .
CATHERINE. Oh, Eve. It's just a dance. What's it matter
who it's with? Besides, you'd rather have me dancing with the
landscape.
EVE. I never meant to say that.
ROY. (*Off.*) I'm coming up.
EVE. I'll break your nose, Roy! (*To Catherine.*) It's just that
it takes time to learn men. They're tricky. It's not a natural
relationship.
ROY. (*Off.*) I'm coming up! (*The bar door opens and closes.
We hear Tammy Wynette, singing, "Stand by your man."*)*
EVE. Roy! No—Roy! Damn. You don't know what you're in
for, little lady. You're about to dance with the least in-
teresting man on the Gulf Coast.
CATHERINE. He can't be that bad, can he? (*Eve stares at
Catherine*) Really?

*See special note on copyright page.

EVE. (*Going to the door.*) I'll go see if I can head him off.
Save you from yourself.
CATHERINE. Well . . . don't lie.

41

EVE. Sure, honey. You just be a little more careful in the future.

CATHERINE. (*As she turns to go.*) Um, Eve? In case someone else asks me, another time . . .

EVE. Yeah?

CATHERINE. Well, could you do me a favor? Could you teach me to dance?

EVE. I'll think about it. (*She turns again to go, stops when she hears a male voice from inside.*)

VOICE. (*Off.*) Can I come out?

CATHERINE. Oh, well—I'm not really sure I want to dance . . . (*Jason enters.*)

JASON. Who asked you?

EVE. Jay Bob! What are you doing up here?

JASON. Nothing. It's my house. Till tomorrow, anyway. (*He moves around the perimeter of the deck, nervously looking down to the street.*)

EVE. Jay Bob, I wonder if you'd mind taking a message down to Roy Manual for us.

JASON. No way. I'm on vacation. Besides, he's a jerk.

EVE. I thought you were helping Jim. You all done?

JASON. Yeah, kind of. Jim and me had sort of a fight, and he said I was all done.

EVE. What were you fighting about this time?

JASON. (*Looking over the railing.*) Nothing. Don't tell him I'm up here. I faked like I was running outside. I don't think he's following me.

EVE. What did you do?

JASON. Nothing. I said. He just likes to persecute me. (*Picks up the book.*) "Sexual Advice For Teens." Who's reading this?

CATHERINE. I am.

JASON. They made you read it in the nun place?

CATHERINE. I found it downstairs.

EVE. Will you please tell me what's going on?

JASON. (*Shrugs.*) I don't know; I don't want to talk about it.

EVE. Fine. Then you deal with it, son. I'm going downstairs. (*Eve exits. Jason regards Catherine.*)

JASON. Hey, you look ok in real clothes for once. How come you're not wearing your nun stuff?

CATHERINE. I don't want to talk about it. (*A pause. They look out over the city. The bar door opens. We hear Johnny Cash singing, "Life ain't easy for a boy named Sue,"\* and the door closes. Jason hurries over, looks down, returns.*)

JASON. False alarm. (*They look over the city.*)

CATHERINE. Don't you have something to do?

JASON. I think I'll just hang out. (*A pause.*)

CATHERINE. It's a nice view. You can see most of the city. Isn't it nice?

JASON. It sucks. This whole town sucks. Four billion people all talking like Gomer Pyle.

CATHERINE. Well, it's not Minnesota.

JASON. I'm going back tomorrow. About time.

CATHERINE. I suppose you'll be glad to see your Dad again.

JASON. Anything'd be better than here. Jim is nuts.

CATHERINE. Oh, I don't think he's . . .

JASON. What do you know? You only been here a few hours. I been here all summer. He's nuts. He makes me work in his crumby business. I'm on my vacation, and he makes me push beer cases around in the back room down there. He's a creepoid jerk.

CATHERINE. Well, I wouldn't say that . . .

JASON. 'Course not; you're a nun. Today he told me to move twenty cases of Schlitz from the front wall to the back wall, and restack 'em. It's the same twenty cases I moved from the back wall to the front wall yesterday. He can't decide

\*See special note on copyright page.

43

where they're "the most efficient." Efficient, my roaring butt. I'm going home tomorrow—what the hell do I care where they are?! (*A beat.*) Does swearing bother you?

CATHERINE. I've, uh . . . I've heard worse.

JASON. So, anyway, I'm doing all this work for him, and when I'm done he comes in and looks at it, and says he liked it better the other way. So I dumped three cases of Schlitz on his foot.

CATHERINE. You didn't.

JASON. I sure as hell did. He started screaming like crazy, and threw a bottle at my head. It missed by this much. He could've killed me, the stupid mother. Day before I go home.

CATHERINE. Maybe if you tried talking with him . . .

JASON. Advice for teens, huh? Actually, I didn't feel like waiting around to talk. There were three guys holding him down when I left. Besides, he's killed people. Did you know that?

CATHERINE. No.

JASON. He told me. Said he used to have a son by his first marriage, and the kid was always pissing him off, so he killed him.

CATHERINE. How?

JASON. With a Schlitz bottle.

CATHERINE. That's ridiculous.

JASON. How do you know? He said he did it.

CATHERINE. He was probably just trying to make you behave.

JASON. (*Picking up the flower pot, taking it to the edge of the deck just above the bar door, and sits with it in his lap.*) I behave. I'm a damn good kid. But he's pushed me too far this summer, that's all I can say. Working in the back room—how'm I supposed to meet any girls?

CATHERINE. (*After a pause.*) What are you doing?

JASON. I'm going to wait for him to come out and drop this on his head.

CATHERINE. Jason!

JASON. Jay Bob.

CATHERINE. Jay Bob, you are not. That's absurd. Put that down.

JASON. You know, that's the only thing Jim ever did I liked. Started calling me Jay Bob. Jay Bob is just as stupid a name as Jason, but at least you can claim your folks didn't know any better.

CATHERINE. Look, um, Jay Bob—why do something like this? You're going home tomorrow. You'll be with your Dad again.

JASON. So what? He's not much better than Jim. Always talking to me about Latvia. He talks in a foreign language like 80% of the time. Nah, it doesn't matter where I am. I'm caught in a war between the generations.

CATHERINE. How about your mother? Don't you care about her?

JASON. She sleeps with Jim. Before that she slept with Dad. I mean, it's a pattern, you know? I know what side she's on. Go back and read your book. Don't mind me—I'll be all right.

CATHERINE. I'm going down and tell Eve.

JASON. You do and I'll drop something on you.

CATHERINE. Jason, it's my duty to warn you that Roy Manual may be up here any minute.

JASON. Roy Manual? Why's he coming up?

CATHERINE. He wants to dance with me.

JASON. What do you want to dance with him for? He's the biggest dipstick in Houston.

CATHERINE. So I'm told.

JASON. Besides, you're a nun. You can't dance. There's a commandment about it or something.

CATHERINE. Well . . . I left the convent.

JASON. How come?

CATHERINE. It's a long story.

JASON. You're not a nun then, huh? You're just, like—

45

what—like nobody, right?

CATHERINE. Pretty much.

JASON. (*Considers this, puts the flower pot aside, stands.*) You wanna dance?

CATHERINE. What?

JASON. Come on, if you wanna dance, dance with me. I'm a lot better than Roy Manual.

CATHERINE. What happened to the war between the generations?

JASON. It'll wait.

CATHERINE. Jason . . .

JASON. Jay Bob. Come on—you're not a nun anymore. Hey—that's good; that's like an oldie. (*Dancing with her momentarily, singing part of the chant from "I want to be Bobby's girl."\**) "You're not a nun any-more . . ."

CATHERINE. (*Breaking away.*) I'm your *cousin*, is what I am.

JASON. You're not that much older than me.

CATHERINE. Jay Bob. Listen to me. I—am—your—cousin.

JASON. So? There won't be all that getting-to-know-you crap. Come on, I've been trying to meet girls all summer. Everybody here talks like hicks. (*Approaching her again.*) Come on, we'll do a close number. I'll sing. (*Softly.*) "You're not a nun any-more . . ."

CATHERINE. (*Breaks away.*) No! I'm going to tell your mother.

JASON. You a virgin?

CATHERINE. Jay Bob!

JASON. I am. I'm not ashamed to admit it. I've been saving myself. I get a feeling you have, too. Is that true? If we want, we could do something about it.

CATHERINE. *You shut up! Right now! Shame on you!* (*She slaps him hard.*)

JASON. (*Beginning to cry.*) Why'd you hit me? Geez!

*See special note on copyright page.

CATHERINE. You are the most offensive teenager I've ever known!

JASON. (*Still in pain.*) *Geez!*

CATHERINE. Well, don't cry . . .

JASON. I'm not crying! Damn grownup. Why's everybody always trying to hit me?

CATHERINE. Well, you were being so . . . aggressive.

JASON. I'm supposed to be aggressive. They said to be aggressive.

CATHERINE. Who? Who said?

JASON. The book I read.

CATHERINE. What book?

JASON. (*Pointing.*) *That* book! "Sexual Advice For Teens." Dating chapter. You just haven't gotten there yet.

CATHERINE. They said to be aggressive?

JASON. Well, kind of aggressive. I don't know. I never picked up a girl before. 'Course I'm not going to do it right the first time. *Geez!!*

CATHERINE. I'm sorry . . .

JASON. I'll be glad to get back to Latvia! (*He moves to the door, and just as he gets there Roy Manual appears.*)

ROY. Hey, there. It's me, Roy Manual.

JASON. (*Taking one look at him, exiting into the house.*) *Geez!*

ROY. What's wrong with him?

CATHERINE. (*Releasing pent-up anger.*) *That stupid little kid!* Eve was right — I've never met any children, that's why I like them. I'm going back to the convent, that's all there is to it. I'll beg them to take me back. I'm not ready for the world again.

ROY. (*Cheerfully.*) Yeah, it's a bitch, ain't it? (*She glowers at him.*) Eve told me about your situation. Must take a lot of courage to leave your order like that.

CATHERINE. I didn't have much choice.

ROY. Still, to get back out in the world, take a look around, try and get used to things again — must take a bunch of guts.

CATHERINE. A bunch of guts?

ROY. Well, you know what I mean. I don't always express it. Did you notice me sitting down there in the bar when you came in this morning? I noticed you. Right away. Been down there ever since, hoping I'd see you again.

CATHERINE. In the bar?

ROY. (*Embarrassed laugh.*) Yeah. I ain't been drinking, though. I been thinking. Thinking there's not many times in a man's life when his whole future suddenly walks by, lighting up the room around her as she goes. That room's still glowing, you should see it.

CATHERINE. (*Looking at him.*) What do you do for a living?

ROY. Nothing. I mean, I'm between work. I'm normally in the trenches, though. (*Laughs.*) That makes me sound like General Patton, don't it? What I mean is, utility trenches. Gas, sewer, water, underground cable — like that. I dig 'em all. But right now I'm not digging, 'cause a little while back I got buried.

CATHERINE. Buried?

ROY. Yeah. Bunch of sand, gravel — happens all the time. I was buried maybe, oh, forty-five minutes? Couldn't get any oxygen for awhile. When they got me out my brain quit working for about three weeks. (*A pause. She regards him. He smiles.*) It's working again now, though. Honest. Better'n before, in fact. I go back on the job next week. (*Slight pause.*) It's a good brain. I'm going to college with it. Community college. Do you like me so far? I always tell too much about myself at the start, don't you think?

CATHERINE. Roy, I'm not sure I feel like dancing tonight . . .

ROY. Well, that's ok. That was just a suggestion. Dancing's just an ice-breaker anyway. Just a way to talk, and . . . stand next to each other, and . . . smell each other's perfume, and — well, I mean your perfume, of course, and my . . .

Well, each other's *scent* is what I'm trying to say. Scent.
CATHERINE. (*Sitting on the chaise.*) Maybe we could just talk.
ROY. Sure, fine. Just talk, great. No problem there. (*He sits next to her. A silence. He pulls out a package.*) Beer nuts?
CATHERINE. (*Shaking her head.*) I wonder where Eve went.
ROY. Eva June? I think there was some ruckus with Jim or something. She went to talk to him. They're a fine couple, ain't they? That Jim is lucky. Always was. Inherited a great place like this bar. Jim Stool's Bar — that's what they used to call it. (*Laughs.*) Used to have a slogan, too: "Other towns got barstools, but only we got Stool's Bar." (*Catherine buries her face in her hands.*) Something wrong? You don't like the joke, huh? Well, the place has a new name now, anyway. (*A pause.*) So, uh . . . suppose it's been hard, having a spiritual failure the way you did.
CATHERINE. (*Angrily.*) It was *not* a failure, it was a . . . (*Pauses, sighs.*) It was a failure. That's exactly what it was. I'm not ready for the world.
ROY. (*Smiling.*) Who is? I know my Daddy always used to say . . .
CATHERINE. (*Rises.*) When I was a little girl, I was offended by human beings. You know that? Literally offended. I was . . . nauseated by the way they watched tv all the time and got married in Las Vegas and built ugly buildings and had mass murders and beat each other up in the park and never even thought about going to church — never sat quietly once and wondered who made their hands, for example, or . . . or anything. You know?
ROY. Kinda. But people get too busy sometimes . . .
CATHERINE. People do not get too busy. They want to get married in Las Vegas, they really do. They want to watch tv — they don't want to watch their hands. Well, I knew that as a kid, and I don't know why but it infuriated me and I had

to be away from it. I had to be a nun. For all the worst reasons. I wasn't attracted to God, I was repelled by the world He made. In a convent there's hardly any world at all, I thought; just a few walls, a few faces. But there was just as much stupidity there—that's what I found out. In those few walls and those few faces there was room for a universe of stupidity. And stupidity is like love, you know?

ROY. I . . . think I do.

CATHERINE. I mean, even the smallest amount of it suggests the whole world. To witness even one act of cruelty or anger or laziness is like . . . like being loved, if only once, by one person, for only a minute. You see? Both things transfigure experience. So that if it's love, let's say, then everything—people, animals, God Himself—everything becomes love, because love, *pure* love, in that lone act, is suddenly seen as possible. Well, the same is true for stupidity. A stupid act will . . . destroy the world someday.

ROY. Not now; they got computers.

CATHERINE. (*With a look at him.*) Because stupidity *does* exist. Everywhere.

ROY. You're well-educated.

CATHERINE. (*Flatly.*) There are some excellent parochial schools.

ROY. You know, I think about religion now and then. (*Pause.*)

CATHERINE. What do you think?

ROY. I think God works in mysterious ways.

CATHERINE. (*Violently.*) Of course He does, as far as you can see! You're stupid! I know exactly how God works. He's created this incomparably lovely, incomparably stupid world for us to live in, and now He sits back and watches us break our hearts over it. I can't imagine how anyone can make love at night and then read the papers the next morning.

ROY. I do that all the time.

CATHERINE. *How?* How can you reconcile the two?

ROY. Making love and reading the paper? (*She nods. He pauses, shrugs.*) I only do the crossword puzzle.
CATHERINE. The murders! Wars! Starvations! What about those?
ROY. They're in another section. I read them later.
CATHERINE. But you read them. And I'll have to, too. You see? I have to remarry the whole world now. (*Points at the city.*) God's world, not the convent, but the world He made, with all the cruelty and despair and deformity and . . .
ROY. (*Standing.*) Are you a virgin?
CATHERINE. Why does everybody want to know if I'm a virgin?!
ROY. You are, ain't you? I could tell. You talk like one.
CATHERINE. Screw you.
ROY. (*Ignoring her.*) And I can see how someone with a virgin nun background the way you got might be taken aback by the world—especially Houston. I mean, it's a pretty wide-open place, isn't it? With some pretty wide-open ways. Hell, I don't know if God made Houston or not. Either way it's a pretty rough and ready town. Got a lot of rough and ready people. (*He is standing right in front of her.*)
CATHERINE. Why are you standing there?
ROY. I want to smell your perfume.
CATHERINE. I'm not wearing . . . (*He kisses her.*) I'm not wearing perfume. (*Roy smiles broadly, lets her go.*)
ROY. I'm not complaining. (*A pause. He smiles again. She turns away. He looks out over the city with pride.*) You know, I don't care if Houston *is* stupid. It's growing like a damn fungus. We can't dig the trenches fast enough. All which ways, too. The city don't know what it's doing anymore—the whole thing's too big for knowing. Guess that's about as stupid as you can get. But we go ahead and dig the trenches, and lay the cables, and fill 'em back in. We figure it's all going to look like something someday. Hell, I

don't even mind if you think I'm stupid, as long as you liked kissing me. You want to go out tomorrow night?

CATHERINE. Roy . . .

ROY. I ain't asking you to remarry the world, just date it a little bit. Come on, what do you say? Tomorrow night?

CATHERINE. Riboflavin.

ROY. What?

CATHERINE. What did I say?

ROY. You said riboflavin.

CATHERINE. I did? Oh, I'm sorry. I meant 100% of minimum daily requirem . . . No—that's not it, is it? I meant smelly butt.

ROY. *What?*

CATHERINE. Smelly butt?

ROY. What the hell are you . . . ?

CATHERINE. What did I just say?

ROY. I don't want to say what you just said.

CATHERINE. Oh no, I'm doing it again.

ROY. What?

CATHERINE. I'm saying odd things. Aren't I?

ROY. You sure are.

CATHERINE. Well, don't take offense. I mean, it's not you or your tiny penis.

ROY. My what?

CATHERINE. (*Distressed.*) I'm doing it again! Why am I doing it again!?

ROY. What are you doing?

CATHERINE. (*Ignoring him.*) I'm not in the convent! I released the pressure.

ROY. Look, if you don't want to go out, just say so. You don't have to . . . (*She barks like a dog.*) What in hell?

CATHERINE. It's nothing. It'll stop. (*She barks again.*)

ROY. Hey, forget I asked you. Don't know where I'd take you anyway.

CATHERINE. (*Very upset.*) Why am I *doing* this?! Because I'm in the world? I can't leave the world. (*Turning to Roy, speaking deliberately*.) Don't worry. I'm under control. My doctor told me to stay calm, and breathe slowly and . . . not talk. (*She sits glumly.*)

ROY. What does not talking do?

CATHERINE. It keeps me from calling you a . . . (*She slaps her hand over her mouth.*)

ROY. I see. You want me to go get Eva June?

CATHERINE. (*Slowly removing her hand.*) No, no. I'll be all right. Just let me rest.

ROY. Ok.

CATHERINE. I'll be fine.

ROY. Good.

CATHERINE. I just need to get used to the world a little more. Too much all at once, I think.

ROY. Would you like a glass of water? (*Jason hurriedly reenters. He is clearly frightened, striving to hide it.*)

JASON. 'Lo again. (*He hurries to the rail above the bar door, looks down.*)

ROY. Hey, Jay Bob. Anything wrong?

JASON. No. Jim's kinda mad again, but . . . Say Roy, could you help me with this? (*Jason starts to lift the flower pot.*)

ROY. What do you want with a dead plant?

CATHERINE. Dead plant?

JASON. Just want to lift it up to the rail here. Come on.

CATHERINE. Jason . . .

JASON. Come on, Roy.

ROY. Well, I don't know . . .

CATHERINE. Jason, put that down.

JASON. *Come on, Roy!* (*The bar door opens. We hear Gogi Grant singing "The Wayward Wind"** for a moment.*)

JASON. Roy!

VOICE. (*Off.*) Jay Bob! Come down here!

ROY. (*Looking over the rail.*) Oh—hey, Jim!

*See special note on copyright page.

JIM. (*Off.*) Jay Bob! You hear me?! (*Pause.*)
JASON. What do you want?
JIM. (*Off, booming.*) *Come down here!* (*A pause.*)
JASON. No.
JIM. (*Off.*) That does it, I'm going to kill him. (*We hear male voices attempting to dissuade Jim.*) No, dammit—he's not getting away with it. Jay Bob—stay right where you are. I'm coming to kill you. (*Sound of male voices again. The bar door opens and closes. Same song. Jason runs to the door, stops.*)
ROY. He don't mean it, Jay Bob.
JASON. How do you know? (*Moving around the perimeter.*) I can't jump; it's too high.
CATHERINE. What's he mad about now?
JASON. Nothing much. I called him kind of a bad name.
CATHERINE. What?
JASON. If I told you, your whole head would probably turn blue, ok? Anyway, he took it wrong. So come on, get me out of here.
CATHERINE. How?
JASON. I'm going up on the roof.
ROY. Need a boost?
JASON. Yeah. (*Just as they begin this, Eve enters.*)
EVE. Where are you going?
JASON. For a walk.
ROY. Hey there, Eva June.
EVE. Shut up, Roy. Get down here. Come on, get down. (*Jason pauses, does so.*) This has gone just about far enough. Where's Jim?
ROY. He's on his way up. He was just down there, and he . . .
EVE. Shut up, Roy. (*To Jason.*) We'll just calmly wait for him to join us, then. (*To Catherine.*) You should've heard what this boy said to Jim. (*To Jason.*) Language has plenty of conventional weapons. I don't know why you always got to

go nuclear with it. (*To Catherine.*) Honey, even you would've been shocked. Things'll be all right, though. I'll calm Jim down. I always do.

ROY. She always does. (*Jim enters. Menacing at his nicest, he is at the moment not very nice. A dark cloud of imminent catastrophe.*) Hey, Jim. How's it going?

JIM. (*Deadly serious, to Jason.*) Take it back.

JASON. What?

JIM. You know what.

EVE. Now Jim, you know I don't like coming between you two, but it seems to me we can talk this over . . .

JIM. You been mouthing me all summer, boy! Now, you got just three seconds to say you're sorry.

JASON. Or what?

JIM. Or you'll die.

ROY. (*With a forced laugh.*) Hey, Jim . . . (*Jim glares at Roy, who shuts up.*)

JASON. You won't kill me. They'd electrocute you.

JIM. It'd be a pleasure, knowing I got you first.

EVE. This is ridiculous. Jay Bob, apologize. That's all he wants.

CATHERINE. Apologize.

JASON. (*Pausing.*) No. I'm on vacation, I don't have to.

JIM. (*Going for him.*) Good enough.

EVE. (*Interposing herself.*) Don't be stupid, Jay Bob.

JASON. (*To Jim with bravado.*) You don't dare kill me!

EVE. That's right, it doesn't make sense. Say you're sorry, Jay Bob.

JASON. Hell I will. I meant every word—you're a low-bellied, puke-faced . . . (*Jim lifts Jason high in the air.*)

JIM. Time's up. (*He takes Jason over to the railing above the bar door.*)

ROY. Hey, Jim . . .

CATHERINE. Jim!

JASON. You're bluffing!

EVE. Set him down, Jim!

JIM. (*To the others.*) Get back! (*They do so. Jim stares at Jason.*) Well?

JASON. You're not a real cowboy. (*Jim throws Jason over the railing.*) Ji-i-i-i-m-m-m-m!!!!!!

EVE. Jason!

CATHERINE. God!

ROY. Hey now! (*They rush to the railing, where Jim has remained. Jim begins a slow, mountainous laughter, as we hear male voices from below hooting with derision.*)

VOICE. (*Off.*) Hey, boys—look who dropped in. It's Jay Bob!

ANOTHER VOICE. (*Off.*) Howdy, Jay Bob. What's the matter? Thought you were gonna die? (*Wild laughter from below. Comments such as "Thought he was gonna die!", "Did you have a good flight?" etc.*)

ROY. A blanket. They caught him in a blanket!

JIM. 'Course they did. You didn't think I was going to kill him, did you?

ROY. Well . . . I wasn't sure . . .

JIM. Hell, he's all right. Hey, Jason—how you doing?

JASON. (*Off.*) You crazy son of a bitch! I'm gonna kill you!

JIM. See? He's fine. Think I'll go down and buy him a drink, now that we understand each other better.

CATHERINE. (*Slowly recovering from her shock, to Jim as he goes.*) You're going to buy him a *drink?* You just threw him off the . . . and now you're going to buy him a drink?

JIM. Why not? He can hold it. Come on, Roy—I'll even treat you. (*Jim and Roy exit.*)

CATHERINE. (*To Eve, who is still looking over the railing, her back to the audience.*) Are you going to let him *do* that? Eve, why don't you say something?

EVE. (*Turning.*) 'Cause I can't stop laughing, that's why. (*Indeed, she is laughing.*)

CATHERINE. Eve!

EVE. Oh, you should see him down there now. I never saw anybody that mad in my life. His face is so red—I wouldn't

56

be surprised if his head explodes.
CATHERINE. I can't believe this!
EVE. What?
CATHERINE. How can you talk that way? That man just threw your son off a balcony.
EVE. So what? He didn't mean to hurt him.
CATHERINE. Jay Bob didn't know that!
EVE. (*Laughing despite herself.*) Well, he knows it now.
CATHERINE. Eve!
EVE. Look, honey. I know how far Jim'll go, and how far he won't go. I admit he had me worried there for a second, but when I looked down and saw Jay Bob bouncing in that blanket — well, it was just funny, you know?
CATHERINE. No. I don't know.
EVE. (*Smiling.*) Don't be a drip. You've never had kids, that's all. My God, I can't tell you how good it felt to see somebody sending that boy over a balcony. About time. I'd've done it myself, 'cept he's been too big ever since he was ten. Hey, come on. Let's go to dinner.
CATHERINE. Dinner?
EVE. Yeah. Aren't you hungry?
CATHERINE. (*Sitting.*) I know what my problem with the world is. I know what it is.
EVE. You do? What is it?
CATHERINE. I'm trying to understand the world. That's my problem.
EVE. Honey, you're just not used to the frontier sense of humor.
CATHERINE. I'm going to forget about trying to understand anything. I'm going to sit here and stare at Houston.
EVE. (*Looking out over the city.*) It gets prettier as the lights come on.
CATHERINE. I mean, why should the world explain itself to me?
EVE. Hell, the world never explains itself. You just gotta make something up. That's what I did. I made up a whole

new way of life. Even built a sign to celebrate the fact: Nice People Dancing To Good Country Music. Hell, you're not doing so bad. You managed to pick out your single favorite person in the whole family, right in the middle of all your trouble. Why not stick with that awhile? You can use Jay Bob's room after tonight. Stay all winter if you want.

CATHERINE. Roy Manual wants to take me out tomorrow. If I don't bark.

EVE. Well go, if you want to. Roy's no fun, but he's no harm either. And you're just starting.

CATHERINE. I think he wants to go dancing. Does it matter if I can't dance?

EVE. With Roy? Nah. Come on—let's get something to eat. (*Catherine smiles, rises. They move towards the door.*) Houston's got a lot of great restaurants. I know a place where the food just fights to get into your mouth.

CATHERINE. Sounds great.

EVE. Yes it is. And we can work more on our men lessons, too. I swear, it's a lifetime study. (*They exit as the bar door opens below. We hear Hank Williams singing, "The silence of a falling star/Lights up the purple sky . . ." and so on from, "I'm So Lonesome I Could Cry."* Slow fade until all we can see is the dimly glowing neon sign. Then it too fades to black.*)

The End

*See special note on copyright page.

58

# INDEPENDENCE

*A Play in Two Acts*

*To Jeanne Blake,*
*the Eugene O'Neill*
*Theater Center*
*and Actors Theatre of Louisville*

*Independence* was given its professional premiere by the Actors Theatre of Louisville during its Eighth Annual Humana Festival of New American Plays in February, 1984. It was directed by Patrick Tovatt; the scenery was designed by Paul Owen; the costumes were designed by Geoffrey T. Cunningham; and the sound design was by James M. Bay. The cast was as follows:

JO............................Shelley Crandall

KESS...........................Deborah Hedwall

SHERRY.............................Gretchen West

EVELYN.............................Sylvia Gassell

*Independence* was developed in workshop at the Cricket Theatre in Minneapolis, Minnesota.

*Independence* was initially presented as a staged reading at the Eugene O'Neill Theater Center's 1983 National Playwrights Conference.

# CHARACTERS

EVELYN BRIGGS . . . . . . . . . . . . . . . . . . . . . . . . . . . . . . 53

KESS . . . . . . . . . . . . . . . . . . . . . . . . . . . . . 33, her daughter

JO . . . . . . . . . . . . . . . . . . . . . . . . . . . . . . 25, her daughter

SHERRY . . . . . . . . . . . . . . . . . . . . . . . . . . . 19, her daughter

# TIME

Late May. The present.

# PLACE

Independence, Iowa.

# ACT ONE
## Scene One

*Interior of an old frame house. Downstage is the living room, Upstage is the front porch. The effect should be of a dark room in the foreground, backed by the bright afternoon sunlight coming through the porch. Right is a door to Sherry's room. Left, a door to the kitchen. Up Right, a hallway leads upstairs. Up Left, an archway leading to the dining room. The living room is filled with old-fashioned furniture: a couch, overstuffed chairs, etc. Well kept up.*

*After a moment, Jo comes through the screen door, onto the porch. She wears an orthopedic collar. Kess follows, carrying a travel bag.*

JO. I can't believe it! You look incredible, you're so tan. How do you get so tan in Minneapolis?

KESS. Jo, shouldn't you be lying down?

JO. Oh, I'm fine. Here, let me take your bag...

KESS. That's ok. I've got it...

JO. *(Entering the living room.)* Well, come on in. Take a look at the old place. What do you think? After four years.

KESS. *(Remaining on the threshold.)* I think you should be lying down.

JO. Don't worry. This is my last day to wear this. The doctor said I'm fine if I don't move fast.

KESS. On the phone you said it was an emergency.

JO. It is an emergency.

63

KESS. You said you were laid up. I came down because I thought you couldn't get out of bed.

JO. I have been laid up. It's just that...

KESS. What do you mean? You're waltzing all over the room. If you've only got a minor injury...

JO. I broke my neck. Well... I chipped it. One of those little bones back there. The doctor said I could have been paralyzed for life. Really. I could have died. *(Of the collar.)* I've had to wear this for a week, I strained the muscles so bad.

KESS. You made me leave my work — you made me drive for hours — because you chipped your neck?

JO. Well ... yes.

KESS. Why?

JO. Are you going to come in or not? *(Kess turns to go.)* Kess! That's not funny. *(Kess stops, looks at her.)* Please come in. *(Kess enters, stands uncomfortably in the room.)*

KESS. How'd you get hurt? *(A beat. Kess turns again for the door.)*

JO. Someone tried to kill me.

KESS. Kill you? Who?

JO. Mom.

KESS. Mom tried to...? Why didn't you tell me on the phone?

JO. I couldn't say it over the phone...

KESS. She tried to *kill* you?

JO. Well, yes... in a way. She hit me. And I fell. I fell six feet. Into the street. You know — over by Duman's Drug? Where the street goes down? It's a six-foot drop from the sidewalk, and ... she pushed me.

KESS. You said she hit you.

JO. She did hit me, but it was like a push. I mean, I fell over backwards. On my neck. I was almost hit by a Plymouth. I didn't wake up for a couple of minutes.

KESS. Did they see it? The person in the Plymouth?

JO. No, they were coming around the corner.

KESS. Did anybody see it?

JO. No, it was Sunday. The stores were closed. But it

happened.

KESS. Why would Mom hit you?

JO. Because I'm pregnant. *(A beat.)* How do you like the house? We painted it last year. *(Kess moves to a chair, puts down her bag, but remains standing.)*

KESS. It's great to be home. I can only stay a couple days. I'm teaching three different courses...

JO. I don't expect you to stay long — honest. I just need you to be here awhile, for support. I need help with Mom, and ... things. You know Mom.

KESS. Yes, I know Mom.

JO. I need you to ... stand up to her. You know — like last time.

KESS. Last time I committed her for three months. Is that what you're talking about?

JO. Oh, no — no, no, no, no, no, no. No. I don't mean that. I just mean having you back would... help so much. You know, having *all* her daughters here for once, for her to...

KESS. Contend with.

JO. *No*, to ... love. *(Sherry enters from her room with a makeup kit.)*

SHERRY. Hey, is that big sister?

JO. Sherry — thought you were taking a shower.

SHERRY. I will tomorrow. *(Setting up a mirror, taking her brush out of the kit.)* Hi, Kess. How're you? Hope you don't mind if I do this while I say hello. I have to go to work. Nice to see you. *(She begins doing her makeup.)*

KESS. Nice to see you.

SHERRY. How you been the last four years?

KESS. Fine. You?

SHERRY. I'm getting out of school in a couple weeks. At long last. Would you believe it?

KESS. You look different.

SHERRY. I hope so. Christ, I was 15 the last time you saw me. You just here for the day?

KESS. Well...

SHERRY. Stay long enough to catch Mom's act. She's really been lighting up the place lately. Ever since Jo got knocked up. Same routine as with me. Something about unmarried pregnant daughters just rings her bell. Check her out. She'll be back from work in a little while.

JO. *(Moving toward the kitchen.)* Kess, why don't we...

KESS. I didn't know she worked.

SHERRY. *(Laughs.)* Oh, yeah. She volunteers out at the MHI.

KESS. Since when?

SHERRY. Almost a year. Jo got her the job. Didn't you write her about that, Jo? Mom's like this model volunteer out there. She made the local paper and everything. "Former Mental Patient Now Helps Others At Mental Health Institute." You know, one of those articles that makes you feel ten feet tall 'n shit? *Look* at this hair of mine. I gotta work tonight.

KESS. *(To Jo.)* Mom's working with mental patients?

SHERRY. Don't worry. She won't hurt 'em. She's just in the craft center. They don't let her alone with anybody.

JO. She wanted to. I couldn't say no.

SHERRY. Hey, what do you think of the pregnant one here? She tell you all about it?

KESS. Not yet.

SHERRY. It's really ridiculous, believe me. I'm sorry, Jo, but it is. I mean, imagine this: Jo, who's been a virgin practically since pioneer days, finally decided to go out with someone. Did she write you about that? So guess what? She goes out with him and goes out with him. And in the course of human events, she gets pregnant.

JO. His name is Don Orbeck.

SHERRY. Deadeye Don Orbeck.

KESS. *(To Jo.)* Well, what's he like?

SHERRY. He's got a Subaru — that's about it. So anyhow, he offers to marry Jo...

KESS. He wants to marry you?

SHERRY. *Did* want to. Jo said no.

KESS. You didn't want to marry him?

SHERRY. She turned him down.

JO. It would have been selfish. *(They look at her.)* To marry him and leave Mom all alone? He's not going to live with her, you know.

SHERRY. He's not completely stupid.

JO. Besides, I think he was just ... offering. You know, 'cause he felt he had to. *(Sherry has pulled hair out of her brush and thrown it on the floor. Kess bends to pick it up.)*

SHERRY. What are you doing?

KESS. Just...

SHERRY. Are you picking up after me?

KESS. You threw hair on the floor.

SHERRY. Put it back. *(Kess hesitates, then does so.)* I *have* a mother for that. So, anyway — like I say, now Jo's alone and pregnant, and there's this marksman walking around town, beginning to look for other targets.

JO. Sherry.

SHERRY. Well, he is. You know who he's showing up at Popeye's with now?

JO. Who?

SHERRY. You want to go insane? Heidi Joy Duckly.

JO. You're kidding.

SHERRY. Nope. Heidi Joy. *(To Kess.)* She's this blonde dwarf you wouldn't believe. I mean, Don was never too inventive, but *Heidi.* You know what Heidi once said to me out loud? "Women should never complain — that's the man's job." Really. I could've strangled the bitch. *(Kess has by now walked up to the front windows, and looks out.)* So what do you think of Jo's life? Screwed up, huh? And I thought I was in trouble when *I* had a kid...

JO. *(To Sherry.)* You should have let me tell her about Don.

SHERRY. You would've taken all day. Hey, Kess. You like my hair this way?

KESS. What? Oh ... sure.

SHERRY. You're not even looking. What are you looking at?

KESS. The traffic light.

SHERRY. *The* traffic light. That's about it. Independence, Iowa.

KESS. Same houses. Even the same billboards.

SHERRY. Only so many ways to sell herbicide. I'll be out of here so fast when I graduate. I'm 19 years old and still in high school. That's the real cost of illegitimate kids, believe me. Jo, you were smart to wait.

KESS. I can see the MHI from here.

SHERRY. Second home to the demented of northeast Iowa. And I do mean Mom and Jo.

JO. Sherry...

SHERRY. *(Rising, after packing up her kit.)* I don't mean it. Just that anybody who works out there is bound to bring some of it home with her.

JO. I work in accounts. I never go near the patients.

KESS. *(Looking off to the side.)* Mrs. Anderberg's collection has grown.

SHERRY. Yeah. Lawn Ornament Land. She must have twenty of 'em out there. All the Iowa standards: stable boys, little fawns, sleeping Mexicans... Hey! You know what? I could use those in a sculpture, I bet. You know — just mush 'em all together some way? Shit, what a great idea. I wonder if I could buy some of them off her tomorrow? I'm an artist.

KESS. Oh? That's nice.

SHERRY. No, really. I won a thing at school. I'm a killer. Even my teacher thinks so.

KESS. That's excellent. I'm impressed.

SHERRY. "That's excellent. I'm impressed." Same old Kess.

JO. Sherry, aren't you late for work?

SHERRY. Don't you wish. Mom and Jo are officially ashamed of me, now that I'm a barmaid at Popeye's.

KESS. Popeye's? Doesn't the school get mad?

SHERRY. Nah. They're too desperate to get rid of me. I graduate in three weeks. *(Taking her kit into her room.)* Hey, how do you like this? I moved downstairs. It's not exactly a separate apartment, but almost. I still think my big mistake was not getting a separate apartment at birth.

KESS. Sherry?

SHERRY. *(Off.)* What?

KESS. How do you think Mom's doing?

SHERRY. *(Returning with a light jacket.)* Oh, fine. Never better. Last night she threw her shoe at my boyfriend. We were sitting in the den, watching tv. Mom was in there, sewing. Me and this guy were hugging and shit — nothing special. Suddenly she chucked her loafer at him. Then she went back to sewing, no explanation. She's great.

KESS. How did Jo get hurt?

JO. I told you...

SHERRY. Mom shoved her off the sidewalk or something, I don't know. Something lame like that. Hey, I gotta go work. Popeye's is sleazy, but it's all money. *(She moves toward the front door.)* Tell me about yourself sometime. See you later. 'Night. *(Stops again.)* This place seem any different to you?

KESS. Yes. A little.

SHERRY. It's not. *(She exits out the front door.)*

KESS. Well. She sure hasn't changed, has she?

JO. Not much. *(Jo picks up the hair on the floor, disposes of it.)*

KESS. So. Mom is not happy.

JO. She's been terrible. Even after I told her I wasn't going to marry Don — that I was going to stay here. She acts like she doesn't believe me.

KESS. Do you think about leaving her?

JO. I couldn't leave her.

KESS. I did.

JO. You're you. You could do that.

KESS. Everyone does that. People grow up. They leave home. *(During Jo's next speech, Evelyn appears unnoticed in the dining room. She wears a coat. She stops when she sees Kess.)*

JO. They don't leave homes like this one. Mom needs more help than other people. She needs someone to be here. Steadily.

KESS. You, you mean?

JO. Well, yes me. If no one else is going to do it. *(A beat.)* I'm sorry.

She still hasn't forgiven you, you know.

EVELYN. *(Moving into the living room.)* Who says I haven't forgiven her?

JO. Mom!

EVELYN. It's silly to say that I haven't forgiven Kess. Where did you get that idea?

JO. Well ... you said...

EVELYN. *(Coming to Kess.)* I can't tell you how surprised I felt when Jo told me you were coming. I hope you'll feel comfortable here.

KESS. Thanks.

EVELYN. Do you want some tea?

KESS. No, thanks.

EVELYN. No? Coffee? Anything?

KESS. No.

EVELYN. Well, I'd like some tea. Jo, why don't you be good and make us some, all right? The way we like it?

JO. Oh ... um, ok. *(She exits to the kitchen.)*

EVELYN. Have a seat.

KESS. In a minute.

EVELYN. *(Sitting near Kess's bag.)* I will. I've been standing for hours. Out at the MHI. I work in the craft center, you know.

KESS. I heard.

EVELYN. I thought you'd be interested, since you were the one who brought me out there in the first place. Of course, now I'm helping other people, instead of being helped. They all like the projects I think up. Just simple things, really. Wood and yarn and paint and things. *(Evelyn opens Kess's bag and rummages inside.)* How long are you staying? Did you bring a lot with you?

KESS. What are you doing?

EVELYN. Looking at your things. *(Holding up a book.)* What's this book? It's awfully thick.

KESS. It's a study of imagery in 17th-Century Scottish Border Ballads.

EVELYN. What do you use it for? Do you read it?

KESS. I'm writing a book of my own.

EVELYN. Really? What's your book called?

KESS. "Imagery in 17th-Century Scottish Border Ballads."

EVELYN. Isn't that the same thing?

KESS. It's my view.

EVELYN. *(Laughs, continues rummaging.)* I'll never understand it.

KESS. Mom, why are you going through my things?

EVELYN. I haven't seen you. I'm trying to get an idea of who you are. How you've changed, I mean.

KESS. *(Retrieving her bag, moving it away from her.)* I haven't.

EVELYN. You came back. How long are you staying?

KESS. Jo and I are still talking that one over.

EVELYN. I hope you stay a long time. It's exciting to have all you girls together again. It's a rare treat.

KESS. Jo said you tried to kill her.

EVELYN. Why don't you sit down?

KESS. I'll sit down when I want to sit down.

EVELYN. Are you afraid to sit down? *(A beat. Kess sits in a chair.)* You always used to sit there. *(Kess immediately rises.)* It's so hard to know what to start talking about after four years, isn't it? Are you still a homosexual?

KESS. *(A beat.)* Yes, Mother. I am still a homosexual.

EVELYN. I suppose that'll make it hard for you to give Jo much advice about this Don Orbeck fellow. She's awfully confused right now. She wanted to marry him, but I think I've pointed out the disadvantages of *that*.

KESS. What are they?

EVELYN. Oh — well, everyone counsels against getting married because of an inadvertant pregnancy. I mean, look at my own life. I married Henry Briggs just because we were expecting you, and that didn't work out so wonderfully, did it?

KESS. I guess not.

EVELYN. What is it about the women in this family? We get near a man, and the next thing we know we're pregnant. You're probably right to stay away from men.

KESS. Mom...

71

EVELYN. Are you sure you don't want to sit? I feel like I'm staring up at a big building.

KESS. I'll stand.

EVELYN. I hope you won't do any homosexual things while you're in town. I mean, it's your life, but...

KESS. *(Moving toward the kitchen.)* I wonder if Jo needs help?

EVELYN. Oh, she's gone down to the bakery for some rolls.

KESS. She has?

EVELYN. She always does when she makes tea. It's one of our little sins.

KESS. *(Sighs, perches on the back of a chair.)* Oh.

EVELYN. It's been so long since we've talked. I admit, I wished you dead there for a couple of years, but I'm over that now.

KESS. Mom...

EVELYN. Jo's almost fully recovered, too. From her neck, I mean. So, I guess you'd say we're all doing very well at the...

KESS. Mom, can I say something?

EVELYN. Of course. We're having a talk.

KESS. As I was driving down here, I was talking to myself— I was saying, "Mom's had four years. We both have. Four years of not seeing each other, not talking, not even writing. Maybe things are entirely different by now. Maybe we'll actually find that we've forgotten how we used to talk to each other. Maybe we'll invent a whole new way."

EVELYN. You talk to yourself in the car?

KESS. Why do we get into conversations like this?! Can't you just say, "Hello, Kess — it's nice to see you again"?

EVELYN. No.

KESS. Why not?

EVELYN. Because it isn't.

KESS. *(A beat.)* Why not?

EVELYN. Isn't it obvious? You left this family long ago. You never visited, you never told us anything about your life...

KESS. I was trying to establish something for myself.

EVELYN. And then, four years ago, out of the blue, you came down here and decided I needed medical help.

72

KESS. You did.

EVELYN. In your opinion.

KESS. I found you sitting on the floor behind a chair, wrapped in a blanket.

EVELYN. And you gave me a hug. I remember; it was very sweet. Then you took me out to the MHI, and...

KESS. What did you want me to do? Take you up to Minneapolis with me? You wouldn't go. Quit my job? Move down here?

EVELYN. That could have been a start.

KESS. I'm a professional! I have a career. It takes all my time and energy — all my love to do it well. I'm not a hack teacher somewhere. I'm extremely good at what I do.

EVELYN. I know, dear. You're a specialist.

KESS. You were only in there three months.

EVELYN. How much love would you like, Kess?

KESS. What?

EVELYN. Isn't that what we're talking about? Really? You're not here for Jo. You're here for love. You want some of my love.

KESS. That would be nice.

EVELYN. Well then, it occurs to me we may only be dickering about the amount. You're a specialist; maybe you don't need a lot of love from me. Maybe you only need a tiny bit. I think I could provide that.

KESS. Why did you try to kill Jo?

EVELYN. I didn't. I hit her.

KESS. She thinks you tried to...

EVELYN. You show me one mother who hasn't hit a child.

KESS. *(A beat.)* Well. I'm going to be here for a little while. I think Jo and Sherry could use whatever comfort and protection that would afford.

EVELYN. They do not need protection...

KESS. I think they do. I think they need that, and love.

EVELYN. You are just like Henry Briggs, you know that? Only here when you want to create new tragedies.

KESS. Mom...

EVELYN. You have all his false appeal and his seeming logic. But

73

just like Henry, you become part of this family only when it suits you, and...

KESS. Mother...

EVELYN. And one day you will leave for good. Won't you? Won't you?

KESS. Why did you hit Jo?

EVELYN. I never hit Jo! *(Rising.)* I remember when a mother and daughter could converse like human beings about these things. You ask anybody in Independence about me. They'll say Evelyn Briggs is the sanest, most well-loved one among us. I am wonderful with those patients. I don't know what Jo may have told you, but it's...

KESS. *(Overlapping from "may.")* Jo has only been...

EVELYN. But it's not true! I am perfectly capable of functioning in a warm and loving universe. Which is what I try constantly to create!

JO. *(From off, in the kitchen.)* Mom! I'm back. I got your favorite! Cinnamon rolls!

EVELYN. I'd better go help Jo. Hope you like Constant Comment. *(She exits into the kitchen. Kess looks around the room, sighs and slumps on the arm of the couch. Lights fade to black.)*

# Scene Two

*Saturday morning, two days later. Lights rise to reveal Jo and Sherry. Jo is dressed, Sherry is still in her robe. Jo is singing from a book. She no longer wears the collar.*

JO.
"It fell about the Martinmas
When nights are lang and mirk..."

SHERRY. *(Yawning.)* Swing it, sister.

JO. Sherry.

KESS. *(From the kitchen.)* Don't mind her. Keep going. You're good.

JO. I am not.

KESS. *(Off.)* Yes, you are.

JO. What's "lang and mirk" mean? "When nights are lang and mirk."

KESS. Long and murky — just like it sounds. *(Entering, with two cups of tea, one of which she gives to Jo. Like Jo, she is dressed.)* Martinmas comes in the winter — so, naturally, long, dark nights. Go on. Your accent's great.

SHERRY. Yeah, great.

JO.
"The carline wife's three sons came hame..."

SHERRY. Came *hame?*

KESS. Sherry. It means home. "Carline" means old, by the way.

JO. Old? Carline means old?

KESS. Yup. It's there so we know she can't have any more children. See? Everything in a ballad has a purpose. That's why they're beautiful.

SHERRY. "That's why they're beautiful." Same old Kess. *(Sherry yawns.)*

KESS. Will you quit yawning?

SHERRY. I didn't get much sleep last night. Besides, I always yawn on Saturdays.

KESS. Go on, Jo.

JO. *(Sings.)*
"The carline wife's three sons came hame
And their hats were o' the birk."

SHERRY. What the hell does that mean?

KESS. It means they're dead.

JO. What?

KESS. Her three sons are dead. They're wearing hats made of birch. "Birk" means birch.

SHERRY. Oh, that explains it.

KESS. But there isn't any birch where she lives. And the next verse indicates that while it doesn't grow there, it does grow at the gates of heaven.

JO. *(Beginning to get it.)* So...

KESS. So they're wearing hats made in heaven. See? They're dead. They were lost in a shipwreck three verses ago. Remember?

JO. How do you keep all this straight?

SHERRY. She doesn't. She makes it up.

KESS. The point is, we're dealing with ghosts here. This poor old woman has three sons, and she sends them all out sailing — major mistake — and word comes back they've drowned. Well, she doesn't want to believe *that...*

SHERRY. Why not?

KESS. So, some time later, they show up — surprisingly — and she's wild with joy. My sons are home! She doesn't notice the birch hats.

SHERRY. *I* would notice the birch hats.

KESS. She doesn't. She loves them, and she can't bear to think they're dead. So she welcomes them, and then she sits and watches over them all night long. But just before dawn she falls asleep. And they wake up before she does, and they leave her forever.

JO. That's awful. I mean it's pretty, but it's awful.

KESS. They can't help it. They have to get back to their graves.

SHERRY. Think I'll have an omelet.

JO. You always have an omelet.

SHERRY. It's all I can cook.

JO. Do you have any more songs?

KESS. Well, here's one about two crows eating a corpse...

JO. Oh ... not yet. Let me work up to that.

SHERRY. Seriously — who wants an omelet?

KESS. What kind?

SHERRY. Plain or lunchmeat.

KESS. No thanks. *(As Sherry exits into the kitchen.)* I'll make breakfast later. Are you taking those vitamins I gave you?

JO. Yeah.

KESS. How's the neck?

JO. *(Turning her head.)* 100%

KESS. Did you throw up today?

JO. Yup.

KESS. Good. We've got all sorts of progress in just two days. Now all we have to do is get you out exercising, instead of sitting around here all day reading drugstore novels.

JO. *Noble Incest* is not a drugstore novel. It's not a great novel...

KESS. We'll see if we can't find you something better.

JO. Kess? Is it fun? To be back?

KESS. Back with you? Yeah, sure it's fun.

JO. How about the town? The people?

KESS. This town? These people?

JO. Yeah.

KESS. Small-town living isn't for me.

JO. I think small towns are an important alternative to the stress of contemporary urban life.

KESS. *(Laughs.)* You do, do you?

JO. How long can you stay?

KESS. I told you. Till Monday.

JO. It's been such a relief to have you here. I really feel calm now. Mom's happier.

KESS. Not sure I believe *that.*

JO. She is. Really. Yesterday she said it's a lovely thing when a family reunites.

KESS. She didn't say it to me.

JO. But she said it. To somebody. That's progress.

KESS. You think that's progress, eh?

JO. Of course it is. It's not easy for her, you know. She has to go by little steps.

KESS. You know what I'd call progress? Real progress? If you were to decide — now that you're going to have a baby — to move up to Minneapolis with me.

JO. What?

KESS. Come and live with me.

77

JO. I couldn't do that.

KESS. Why not? Try and think about it rationally...

JO. I don't have to think about it rationally. I couldn't do that.

KESS. Why not?

JO. 'Cause I can't leave Mom. How can you even suggest it?

KESS. I'm only...

JO. What would happen to her? Tell me — what would happen?

KESS. She'd be all right.

JO. She would, huh? How?!

KESS. She's managed for 53 years.

JO. No, she hasn't. She's never managed alone. She's always needed someone. First there was her family, then Dad, then you after Dad left, then me. Who'd be here when I left? Not Sherry. Mom would be all alone.

KESS. *(A beat.)* So what?

JO. *So what?!*

KESS. I have a very big place in Minneapolis. There'd be room for you. My roommate wouldn't mind...

JO. You already asked your *roommate?* Jesus, Kess...

KESS. I had to know before I could...

JO. Is that the only reason you came down? To try and steal me away from Mom?

KESS. No, it's just that...

JO. If you think I'd leave Mom to move up there with you and that ... that...

KESS. That what?

JO. You know.

KESS. That what? That Susan, you mean. That's her name.

JO. I think we should just drop it.

KESS. *(With control, not defensive.) That* roommate — Susan — is the same as me. Our life is more normal than anything that goes on in this house.

SHERRY. *(Off.)* That's the truth.

KESS. Sher, if you want to join the conversation you can come in here.

SHERRY. *(Off.)* No, thanks.

JO. *(A beat.)* I'm sorry.

KESS. That's all right.

JO. I just know I can't go up there and leave Mom, that's all.

KESS. 'Cause she needs you.

JO. That's right.

KESS. What for? What does she need you for?

JO. Everything. She needs me to listen to her. She needs me to talk to her, to be with her — to be thinking about her. What does anybody need anybody for?

KESS. Shouldn't people sometimes ... change who they need?

JO. Mom's done that.

KESS. I don't mean Mom. I mean you.

JO. *(A beat.)* We're getting off the point.

KESS. What do you need from Mom?

JO. Nothing. I help her. She doesn't help me. Ok?

KESS. Something. You get something out of it.

JO. I don't get a thing. I give. That's my life. I give to people. There's nothing wrong with it. You should try it sometime.

KESS. I wasn't saying...

JO. It's easy for you. You just take what you need from people. You don't care how much you change in the process. You don't care if your whole family doesn't recognize you anymore when you... *(She stops herself, very embarrassed.)* I'm sorry.

KESS. That's all right.

JO. It's not true — we recognize you. You're always ... Kess. *(A beat. Kess sighs.)*

KESS. Well...

JO. Why don't you move down here?

KESS. What?

JO. Move back down. Be close to us.

KESS. I couldn't do that.

JO. Why not? You make changes. You could find a way. Bring Susan.

KESS. *Su*san...? Mom'd *love* that.

JO. You could work, you could find a job...

KESS. Jo ...

JO. You can do anything if you care enough.

KESS. Is that why you asked me down here? To steal me away from my life?

JO. I'm not stealing you away! I'm ... inviting you. You could do a lot of good down here. You could really provide something for Mom...

KESS. I do provide. I provide a hell of a lot, as you'll recall. Who was here to put Mom in the MHI when she needed it?

JO. Who was here when she got out? You were already gone. I was the one who took her around to say hello to everybody again. I took her into each store. I shopped with her.

KESS. I'm leaving on Monday.

JO. Go ahead — leave!

KESS. I will.

JO. Fine! *(A silence. Sherry enters, eating a Hostess Cupcake.)*

SHERRY. How are things in here? Everybody happy?

KESS. I thought you were having an omelet. What's that?

SHERRY. Dessert. This is getting to be a lively day. What with you guys yelling, and Mom.

KESS. What about Mom?

SHERRY. You didn't hear her dawn raid this morning? It was a beaut. She caught me with a boy.

JO. She's caught you with boys before.

SHERRY. Not with two boys.

JO. *Two* boys...?

SHERRY. Oh, it was just inane. I was only in bed with one of them.

JO. Well, who...?

SHERRY. Ed and Red Randall. *(To Kess.)* Ed's my boyfriend.

JO. What was Red doing there?

SHERRY. He came over to ask Ed a question, that's all. I think he wanted to borrow money, I don't know. It was still dark out. Anyway — it was so stupid — Red was crawling through the window, and he slipped on my dresser and made this incredible crash, and Mom came in. And there we were: all three of us on the bed. Well,

80

Red was kind of half on the floor.

JO. Oh, Sherry...

SHERRY. Mom must've been wandering around out here. She came right in, she was all dressed and everything. Anyway, she practically killed Ed and Red, thereby ruining my social life.

JO. What'd she do?

SHERRY. *(Laughs.)* She threw your picture at them. You know — your graduation picture. In the frame? *(Sherry points to a table where Kess and Sherry's framed pictures sit, with a noticeable gap between them.)*

JO. Oh, no.

SHERRY. Who knows why she was carrying it around with her?

JO. Where is it now?

SHERRY. All over my room. They were both scared shitless. They were out the window in two seconds. Then she screamed, "You'll thank me someday," and ran out.

JO. Where'd she go?

SHERRY. Who knows? Maybe she went and drowned herself.

JO. I'll check her room. *(Jo hurries upstairs.)*

KESS. Why didn't you tell us about this?

SHERRY. What's to tell? It's the way she always is.

KESS. Don't you care about her at all?

SHERRY. Don't you? I don't see you running upstairs. *(A moment passes. Jo returns.)*

JO. She's ... asleep. She's fine.

SHERRY. She's fine and Ed's terrified. *(Curling up on the couch.)* Be sure and tell me when you both finally sneak out on her for good. I don't want to be the last one out the door. *(She closes her eyes, napping. The others stare at her, then at each other. Lights fade to black.)*

# Scene Three

*Around noon, the same day. Jo is staring out a side window, toward the back of the house. We hear sweeping sounds from Sherry's room. After a moment, Evelyn emerges — a dustpan full of glass in one hand, a broom and a damaged photo in the other.*

EVELYN. That takes care of that. At least your photo wasn't too badly torn. A little scotch tape... *(Evelyn moves toward the kitchen with the dustpan.)*

JO. I'm sorry you had to clean it up yourself.

EVELYN. No— Sherry has every right to demand that. I was the one who lost her temper. I made the mess. *(Evelyn disappears into the kitchen.)*

JO. She wouldn't let me clean it up. I offered to, but she just...

EVELYN. *(Off.)* It's fine, it's fine. Your heart was in the right place. *(Reentering, sans broom and dustpan, but with the picture.)* Have to get a new frame for this. *(Sets it on the table with the other photos.)* Such a sweet picture. I'm sorry it was yours I threw. But I was looking at it right when I heard those noises, and I just...

JO. That's ok, Mom.

EVELYN. Well, there's a basic level of trust. In any home.

JO. I know. Did you sleep well, this morning?

EVELYN. Like a dream. Lost half the day, but I don't care. Is Sherry around? Where is everyone?

JO. Kess went out for a run. Sherry's in the backyard.

EVELYN. *(Moving to the window Jo had been looking out.)* She is? What's she doing?

JO. Working on her sculpture.

EVELYN. Oh. Well. She should stop it.

JO. Tell her that.

EVELYN. It's so awful. And it's right next to Mrs. Anderberg's vegetable garden. She called and complained yesterday. Said if she'd only known what Sherry was going to do with those lawn ornaments, she'd never have sold them to her.

JO. Too late.

EVELYN. I said if she wanted to go ahead and sue Sherry, I'd back her up.

JO. Against your own daughter?

EVELYN. I'm not really sure Sherry is my daughter. I was so drugged up when I had her, they could've given me any baby and I wouldn't have known. *(Jo laughs. Evelyn smiles.)* It's nice, having you all in the house again. We're never all together in the same room, it seems, but at least we're all ... around. Do you like having her here?

JO. Who — Kess? Sure. It's wonderful.

EVELYN. *(A beat.)* It is, isn't it.

JO. Yes, it is.

EVELYN. I hope she's having a good time. I suppose she probably came down here expecting to find us locked in some sort of death struggle.

JO. She did not.

EVELYN. Lord knows what you told her.

JO. I didn't tell her anything.

EVELYN. You told her I hit you.

JO. You did hit me.

EVELYN. I did not. I struck out, that's all. I simply struck out against Fate, and there you were. It's not the same as hitting.

JO. It *felt* the...

EVELYN. It's not the same. *(A beat.)* There's not the same responsibility, is there?

JO. *(A beat.)* No.

EVELYN. *(Picking up a magazine.)* Kess has been talking to people in town about me. Did you know that? Mrs. Herold was angry about it. She really was. Kess walked up to her — hadn't seen her in years — and said, "How does my mother seem to you these days?". I can just hear her.

JO. I'm sure she didn't mean anything...

EVELYN. If I hadn't had the three of you so far apart we'd be more of a family. There'd be more of us in the room right now. Kess was nearly grown by the time Sherry was born. They must stare at each other like the Earth and the moon.

JO. Do you want some lunch...? *(Evelyn puts the magazine down.)*

EVELYN. Where were you Wednesday night?

JO. What?

EVELYN. Wednesday night. The night before Kess got here. Where did you go?

JO. Nowhere important.

EVELYN. Where, though?

JO. Nowhere.

EVELYN. You must've gone somewhere.

JO. I didn't go anywhere, all right? I really didn't.

EVELYN. I'm only curious.

JO. What's it matter?

EVELYN. I guess it doesn't.

JO. That's right. It doesn't matter. It doesn't matter at all.

EVELYN. *(A beat.)* Then why can't you tell me?

JO. *(Moving toward the stairs.)* I'm going to go change. Kess and I are going out when she gets back...

EVELYN. Mrs. Rowley says she saw you over at Don's house Wednesday night. *(Jo stops.)* Is that where you were? Don's house?

JO. Yes.

EVELYN. You went over there, and you never told me?

JO. There was nothing to tell. He wasn't home.

EVELYN. Oh. You were gone a long time.

JO. I know. I just ... sort of sat on his step for awhile.

EVELYN. *(A beat.)* Why?

JO. I ... thought he might come home.

EVELYN. No — I mean, why did you go see him?

JO. No reason.

EVELYN. There's always some reason. There must have been

some reason.

JO. I wanted to see if he felt like going out, all right?

EVELYN. You didn't call him first?

JO. It was kind of a whim.

EVELYN. I thought you and Don were finished.

JO. We are; so what? *(A beat.)* He's dating other people. I sat for half an hour on his step. Folks walked by and said, "Hi, Jo. Don's out tonight, you know." I said, "I know." They all looked at me like I was ... what I was. So I came home.

EVELYN. *(Moving to her, sitting close.)* I've missed you these last weeks. I'm glad we're not fighting anymore. Aren't you? *(Jo nods. Evelyn takes her hand.)* Sometimes a man comes into your life, and you think it's the answer to your problems, but you always find out it's not. Henry was just a man. He didn't care about me. He was handsome, and he was fine while there was enough money, or there was enough whatever, but in the end he didn't care.

JO. I know.

EVELYN. I'll be glad when Sherry's gone. I shouldn't say that, but I will. Then it'll just be you and me. Won't that be fun? *(Jo nods.)* We'll have Kess and Sherry visit now and then, of course. But mostly, it'll just be us. I rely on you. So few people in the world can really be relied on. Don't you think? So few things. I've lived in this house my entire life. Do you realize that?

JO. It amazes me sometimes.

EVELYN. You too. You've lived in it all yours.

JO. Yes.

EVELYN. Kess will be gone on Monday. Then Sherry will go. Just you and me. At last. *(A beat.)* I'm wearing my cameo.

JO. What?

EVELYN. I'm wearing my cameo. Did you notice?

JO. Oh ... it's lovely. I'm sorry, I didn't notice.

EVELYN. That's because you haven't been looking at me. In the craft center they tell us to look squarely at the patients — at least at those who'll look squarely at us — and to smile, and to be encouraging. I think that's good advice for life in general, don't you? *(Of the cameo.)* It's a beautiful thing, isn't it? Family heirlooms always are.

JO. Yes.

EVELYN. Henry, your father, and I used to drive to Des Moines once a month when you were little. He went on business — allegedly — and I went to shop. After we'd done this for over a year, he suddenly looked at me on the way home one day and said, "What's that?". I said, "It's my cameo." "Where did you get it?" he asked. "I've had it for seven years," I told him. "Why haven't you ever worn it before?". "I wear it all the time," I said, "It's my dearest possession." He was just silent then, the whole way home. Never said he was sorry. *(Unpinning the cameo, examining it.)* That was the first time I ever felt sorry for him, though. Must be strange for a man, to live in a world full of only big things.

JO. You used to show it to Kess and me.

EVELYN. I did, didn't I?

JO. You let us hold it.

EVELYN. *(Starts to hand it to Jo, then suddenly pulls it back for reexamination.)* You two fought over it. Didn't you?

JO. Some fight. Kess always won. *(Evelyn pins the cameo back on herself.)* You haven't had it on in ages. Why are you wearing it now?

EVELYN. So I don't forget to give it to Kess.

JO. You're giving it to Kess?

EVELYN. Well, I know I talked about giving it to you. But that was when I was mad at Kess, and thought she wasn't a part of us anymore.

JO. Kess is getting the...?

EVELYN. You know, I thought of it just as I woke up. It's truly the perfect idea. After all, Kess has been so much calmer this trip. We need to give her something. And what better than the cameo? It's hers by rights. She is the oldest.

JO. But...

EVELYN. I know — I'm breaking tradition, to give it to her before I die. But I thought it might be just the message she needs to see that ... I love her, and I'm all right. Do you think she'll like it?

JO. *(A beat.)* Of course. It's lovely.

EVELYN. It is, isn't it? I remember when your Aunt Elaine died, and I got it. Do you realize this cameo has been owned by women in our family for over 150 years? Imagine. I'm sorry I don't have one for you, too. But Kess has to live far away. We can give her this to remind her of us. You're right here. You have me. *(A beat.)* I'll tell you something else. Now that Don is... well, moving in another direction, I think you and I have a special opportunity — one that a mother and daughter rarely get. We have the chance to give each other something far more valuable than a cameo.

JO. What?

EVELYN. Our lives. *(A long beat. Evelyn kisses Jo on the forehead. Jo is motionless.)* Now, where can I leave this?

JO. Leave it?

EVELYN. I know! On her table upstairs. She'll find it when she goes up tonight. *(She goes for the stairs.)*

JO. Well ... if you're going to give it to her, why don't you give it to her?

EVELYN. No, no, no. This is better. A surprise.

JO. It's ridiculous, giving her the cameo like that.

EVELYN. You don't understand — it'll be lovely. Look: I sneak in her room, leave it on her table. She walks in, wanders around, comes over to the table and... You see? It'll be very special.

JO. That's not special.

EVELYN. Of course it is.

JO. Putting it in her hand and looking her in the eye — that would be special. Leaving it on a table is lousy.

EVELYN. No, it's lovely. You just don't see it.

JO. I would never want to get a gift that way. Especially that gift. From my own mother...

EVELYN. Kess will adore getting this gift in just this way. And no amount of jealous carping...

JO. I'm not jealous! I'm not!

EVELYN. No one knows Kess the way I do. And I am going up this minute and leaving this cameo right on her goddamn table, is that clear?!

JO. Yes.

EVELYN. Good. Kess is my oldest. She and I communicate in ways you and Sherry would not understand.
JO. Yes, Mom. *(Evelyn starts to exit, stops.)*
EVELYN. It will be a lovely gesture. From the both ‹ ꜝ us. *(Evelyn exits upstairs. Jo stares after her a moment, as lights fade to black.)*

# Scene Four

*Sunday evening, the next day. Sherry at a table, with a pile of slides in front of her. She looks at them one by one as she speaks, dividing them into two piles. Kess, wearing the cameo, sits on the couch, looking through a book.*

SHERRY. So what I'm saying is, he was fantastic, that's all.
JO. *(Off, in Sherry's room.)* He was, was he?
SHERRY. Of course he was. He's from New York. He's a biker. I met him at the bar last night.
KESS. *(Absently.)* Sounds very attractive.
SHERRY. Yeah, he's an artist.
KESS. *(Calling out.)* How about Standish?
JO. *(Off.)* What?
KESS. Standish. That might be all right.
JO. *(Off.)* Are you kidding? *Standish?*
SHERRY. I can't believe you guys are actually picking baby names.
KESS. We actually are. *(Calling.)* How about Hannibal?
JO. *(Off.)* No. Sherry, where's your black top?
SHERRY. On the closet door.
JO. *(Off.)* Oh — thanks!
SHERRY. *(To Kess.)* Don't you want to hear about this guy I met?
KESS. No. *(Sherry suddenly steals Kess's book.)*
SHERRY. Well, do — 'cause he's real interesting.

KESS. Sherry...!

SHERRY. Come on. You can do baby names later. This guy is a grown-up.

KESS. I don't have time. I'm going home tomorrow.

SHERRY. So what? Mail it in. *(Kess grabs for the book. Sherry pulls it away and sits on it. A standoff.)*

KESS. Jo, she's got the book.

JO. *(Off.)* Sherry...

SHERRY. Jo — try my black shoes, too. They're on the stereo. One of 'em is, anyway.

JO. *(Off.)* Oh — yeah. Thanks!

SHERRY. No problem. *(To Kess.)* So. First of all, he's very aloof. Like he's not from here, right?

KESS. *(Looking irritably at Sherry's room.)* Where's he from?

SHERRY. New York. Don't you listen? Like I said he's a biker.

KESS. Charming.

SHERRY. He's got this great big Harley that looks like it eats rabbits. And he's got leathers and chains... And he's got tattoos.

JO. *(Off.)* Tattoos?

SHERRY. On both arms! Plus a little one on his nose. It's like this little vine or something, curling around one nostril. Want to know what his job is?

KESS. *(Leaning in the doorway to Sherry's room, staring into it.)* No.

JO. *(Off.)* Yes!

SHERRY. He's an insect photographer.

JO. *(Off.)* A what?

SHERRY. He takes close-up shots of insects — like in Walt Disney movies and stuff. He's got this butterfly net on his bike. I saw it.

KESS. Jo, do you really think you should wear that?

JO. *(Entering, wearing a showy black top.)* Why not?

KESS. You don't know what Don's coming over for, exactly.

JO. He's taking me out. He said. "Can we go someplace?" Those were his exact words. Sherry, do you like it?

SHERRY. Yeah, on me. *(A beat. They stare at Jo.)*
JO. Well ... I thought maybe he'll want to go to a restaurant or something. *(A beat. Jo's confidence crumbles. She goes back into Sherry's room.)*
SHERRY. Anyway, this guy's one of Disney's biggest suppliers. That's what he told me, at least. You know what insect he hates to film?
KESS. I give completely up.
SHERRY. The praying mantis.
JO. *(Off.)* What about the green?
KESS. Jo...
SHERRY. He says everybody does that. Every nature movie has a praying mantis in it. You ever notice that?
KESS. Sherry...
SHERRY. And it's always the same shot: praying mantis sits there not moving; praying mantis grabs something faster than you can see it anyway; praying mantis eats it; praying mantis sits there not moving again. It's a limited insect.
JO. *(Off.)* I'm wearing this one.
KESS. I don't think...
JO. *(Off.)* Forget it. My mind's made up.
SHERRY. You know what he likes better? The dung beetle. They're more inventive. They roll these little balls of dung all over hell, you know?
KESS. I know.
SHERRY. They're very creative. Anyway, like I say, this guy's an artist, and I showed him some slides of sculptures I made, and he liked 'em, *and* he's taking 'em to New York with him. To try and make me famous — you know? I'm sending him more tomorrow. Want to see 'em?
KESS. No.
JO. *(Off.)* What's his name?
SHERRY. What?
KESS. Has the Hell's Angel insect photographer art connoisseur got a name?
SHERRY. Spinner. Isn't that great? We only knew each other a

90

couple hours. It was kind of a lightning relationship. *(Hands Kess her book back.)* Just thought you'd be interested. *(Jo reenters in a top that's slightly more demure, but still is too dressy.)*

JO. This is it. How do I look?

SHERRY. Like Heidi Joy Duckly.

JO. Well, I don't care. It's what I'm wearing.

KESS. Jo, you don't even know where you're going.

JO. We're going somewhere. That's all that matters.

KESS. Why not stay here? You two could talk here.

JO. *(Going to the front window, looking out.)* Oh, brilliant idea.

KESS. When's he coming?

JO. A half hour. *(Moving to the couch.)* I can't believe he called. Someone must've told him I was at his house.

SHERRY. Yeah, like half of town.

JO. I don't care.

KESS. Jo, is Don really worth getting this excited about?

JO. I'm not excited.

KESS. It's just that ... for all the trouble he's caused...

JO. What trouble?

KESS. Mom tonight, for one thing.

JO. Well ... I can't help Mom. We already had one fight over it, and that's it. She's all right now.

KESS. She's out cleaning up the garage. At seven in the evening. Does that sound like she's all right?

JO. It's not my fault if she loses her temper! You should be happy I'm getting away from her.

KESS. I am, but...

JO. You're just mad 'cause it's your last night here, and I'm going out. I understand that. And I'm sorry, but...

KESS. I just wish you'd be a little less frantic about it.

JO. How do you expect me to be? Don called up. Maybe he wants to ask me to get married.

SHERRY. What if he does? You'll just say no again.

JO. I will not.

SHERRY. Will he agree to live with Mom? Will he even come in the house?

91

JO. I'll leave Mom.

SHERRY. Sure.

JO. I wish he'd get here.

KESS. Relax.

JO. Maybe he'll take me to a movie. We like doing that. Sher, what's on in town?

SHERRY. The new James Bond.

JO. James Bond! God. Great. Remember when we used to go to those as kids?

KESS. Yeah. Mom used to take us.

SHERRY. Sure. They were the only movies a 20-year-old, a 12-year-old and a 6-year-old all liked.

JO. That's right. Remember, we'd all sit there eating out of those red and white striped popcorn boxes, and Mom would lean over us and say, "Watch James Bond. Watch the way he acts around women. Watch what happens to the women..."

KESS, JO and SHERRY. (Together.) "They al-l-l-l-l-l-l die." (They laugh.)

SHERRY. God, we all remember.

JO. "They al-l-l-l-l-l-l die." Just like that. What happened to the woman in that movie, anyway? Didn't she fall into a car-masher or something?

KESS. I think so.

JO. Yeah. (A beat. They grow silent.)

KESS. (Sighs.) Ok, ok, ok. Go out with him. Have a good time. Get frantic if you want to.

JO. Thanks. So — um... (Indicates the book.) Pick more baby names.

SHERRY. Do we have to?

KESS. All right. What about, um ... Lanier.

JO. Lanier? I don't know.

SHERRY. Could we please do anything else?

KESS. What about Banquo?

JO. Will you quit it?

SHERRY. How about Shulamith?

JO. Give me a girl's name. It's going to be a girl.

SHERRY. Shulamith is a girl's name.

KESS. Let's see: Marina.

JO. No.

KESS. Chloe.

JO. Are you ignoring all the common ones?

KESS. Who needs a book for Mary? Annabella.

SHERRY. Have we really, honestly considered Shulamith?

JO. Sherry...

SHERRY. Hey — how about Merlin?

JO. *Mer*lin? Why?

SHERRY. 'Cause then he could make himself disappear.

JO. He's not going to disappear! He's going to be born, and have a mother and a father!

SHERRY. Yeah, who?

JO. *Me and Don!*

SHERRY. Oh, wake up! He's probably coming over to tell you to keep off his porch!

KESS. Sherry!

SHERRY. And you — you're a bigger idiot than Jo! Picking *baby* names. I noticed you never picked one for mine.

KESS. What good would that have done?

SHERRY. It might've helped me keep it.

KESS. You were 15 years old.

SHERRY. I was old enough! You had to pry it away from me with a stick!

KESS. *I'm glad I had a stick! (A beat. Kess puts down the book.)* Let's not do this.

SHERRY. *(Quietly.)* I gave her a name myself, anyway. Shulamith. 'Course she's probably called Barbie or Cathy by now.

KESS. Wherever she is, she's in a better family than this.

SHERRY. How would you know? You only come down when you feel like it. *(Flicking Kess's cameo.)* You just drop in now and then, pick up whatever you want, and leave.

KESS. Oh — I suppose you wanted it too, huh?

SHERRY. No, but Jo did.

JO. I did not.

KESS. *(To Sherry.)* I come down here because you three can't get along without me. Eventually you always have a disaster.

SHERRY. Maybe we like disasters!

JO. You *guys...*

SHERRY. I can't believe it. You don't care any more about this family than I do — but everybody looks up to you. Everybody's afraid of you. And meanwhile I'm supposed to be this little *shit...*

KESS. Well put! *(Sherry gives an angry yell and pushes Kess onto the couch. They struggle.)*

JO. Kess! Sherry! Stop it!! Let go! LET GO!! *(As they fight, Evelyn enters via the kitchen. She is disheveled, bleeding, frightened.)*

EVELYN. Kess? Kess?

JO. *(Looking around.)* Oh, God — Mom! *(The others look up.)*

EVELYN. Kess, I'm hurt.

JO. *(Rushing to her, as the others rise.)* What happened?

EVELYN. *(Moving into Kess's arms.)* I was cleaning the garage. I ... found the old dishes. The old china. I think I ... broke something. I couldn't hold onto the plates... *(Kess and Jo move her to a chair. Sherry runs out through the kitchen.)*

JO. I'll get a towel. *(Jo exits into the kitchen.)*

EVELYN. There was just me. There was ... I was all alone out there.

KESS. Calm down, now. Everything's all right. You're with me. *(Jo reenters with a towel.)*

EVELYN. I kept seeing Jo. She wasn't ... there, but she ... I saw her.

JO. Are those her only cuts?

KESS. I think so.

JO. Here, let me wrap this around. *(Sherry reenters.)*

SHERRY. Geez — I don't believe it. The garage is full of broken dishes. Everywhere you look.

EVELYN. I was completely alone. *(A car horn honks outside.)*

JO. Oh, God — Don! *(Moving toward the front door.)* Um ... um... *(The horn honks again.)* Kess, I ... that's Don ... I ... *(She suddenly bolts out the front door.)*

EVELYN. Where's she going?

KESS. It's all right.

EVELYN. But where's...?

KESS. Why did you break the dishes?

EVELYN. What?

KESS. Why did you break the dishes?

EVELYN. They were in my hand.

SHERRY. How bad are her cuts?

KESS. Not bad. Mom, were you throwing them at someone?

EVELYN. Yes.

KESS. Who? Who were you throwing them at? *(Jo reenters from the front.)*

JO. Mom? I sent him away. I told him I couldn't see him, all right? Mom? I sent Don away. He's gone. He's all gone.

EVELYN. *(Quietly.)* I threw them at Jo. *(Lights fade to black.)*

## END OF ACT ONE

# ACT TWO
## Scene One

*Lights rise on Kess and Evelyn, in robes, sitting at a table. They are playing* Scrabble. *Late Thursday evening, four days later.*

EVELYN. I used to sit around this table with my own sisters. You know that? I remember many times we'd sit around this same room, and just talk for hours. Mostly about our friends. Well, their friends, really. I was much younger. We'd stay up whole nights. This house. My mother was born in it.

KESS. Do you allow Greek letter words?

EVELYN. Like what?

KESS. Alpha, beta, pi.

EVELYN. No. *(A beat.)* Staying up nights. I always loved that when I was young. Now I wish I could sleep.

KESS. You slept last night, didn't you?

EVELYN. Oh, yes. I'm much calmer than I was. You've been so good to me all week. I'm sorry I made you change your plans, but I'm glad you're staying longer.

KESS. I just want to make sure you're feeling better. I mean, since your...

EVELYN. My smash up? Oh, yes. I feel much better. Actually, that let off a lot of steam for me. I scared myself, I admit, but now I'm almost glad it happened. And I won't miss those dishes. They were terrible old things. You almost make me feel like a princess, you've paid so much attention to me since. I hope it hasn't been hard on you.

KESS. Agony.

EVELYN. Really? That bad?

KESS. *(Putting letters on the board.)* No, that's the word I'm playing. "Agony." Let's see: that's one-two-three-four-five-six-seven-eight-nine. Plus a double word score. Eighteen.

EVELYN. Who's ahead?

KESS. I am.

EVELYN. Really? By how much?

KESS. Um ... 380 points.

EVELYN. Oh... *(Playing.)* "Me." *(Kess looks at her.)* That's what I'm playing.

KESS. *(Recording the score.)* Four points.

EVELYN. I think it's so sweet of you to babysit me while your sisters have a night out.

KESS. They've had three nights out.

EVELYN. Well, they need it. What with Jo having that new disappointment with Don. I think she's lost all her chances there, don't you? You can't keep telling someone to go away, and expect them to keep coming back. Has she tried to call him again?

KESS. *(Nods.)* Mm-hmm. He's never home, though.

EVELYN. Well. We're certainly home, aren't we? Just a couple old maids, home for the night. *(As Kess works out a move.)* How am I?

KESS. What?

EVELYN. Do you think I'm in trouble?

KESS. What do you mean?

EVELYN. In the game.

KESS. Oh — can you win? No, you can't.

EVELYN. Ah. *(A beat.)* Do you like the cameo? I've noticed you wear it a lot.

KESS. It's beautiful. Thanks again.

EVELYN. You're welcome. Is it fun having a family again? It must be wonderful to rediscover your sisters this way. I remember my own sisters. I used to have such sweet memories of them, mostly. *(Indicating the room.)* We used to sleep right in here, sometimes. All of us, together. On hot summer nights. You going to play soon?

KESS. Pretty soon.

EVELYN. We would take sheets — all of us — and we'd open all

97

the windows and the porch door and turn on the fan, and sleep on our wonderful white heaven of bare sheets.

KESS. How about solmizations?

EVELYN. What?

KESS. Do, re, mi, fa, sol...

EVELYN. No, I don't allow those. Anyway, it was such an adventure for me. There I was, the baby of the family, trying to stay awake while they were all trying to go to sleep.

KESS. Uh-huh.

EVELYN. All night I would stare right along the floor, under the davenport. I don't know what I ever expected to see there. And in the morning I'd wake up, and someone would have turned off the fan, and it would be cold some mornings, if a front had gone through. And there I'd be: wrapped in a sheet, with Elaine's — she was my favorite sister — with Elaine's arms around me. That's the loveliest waking-up memory I have, and I was married for almost 16 years.

KESS. Come back to the table.

EVELYN. Have you got a play?

KESS. Just about.

EVELYN. *(Sitting again.)* I think we go at different paces. I like to play a lot of games of *Scrabble* in one sitting. You make each game a work of art.

KESS. *(Playing two letters.)* Let's see ... if I do this, it's four this way for "gal," 35 for "maze," and 37 for "hazel" because of the two triple-letter scores ... which makes a grand total of ... 76.

EVELYN. "Up."

KESS. Four points. Mom, are you enjoying this? We don't have to play if you don't want.

EVELYN. What else would we do?

KESS. Well ... I guess we could play a little longer.

EVELYN. Why not? *(As Kess considers her next move.)* You know, the other night, when I was ... throwing those dishes? I imagined Jo was there.

KESS. I know. You told me.

EVELYN. All around me, sort of. It was her I was throwing the dishes at. I knew I was imagining — I wasn't confused about that. But it was very vividly her. All those dishes.

KESS. Do you really want to go into it?

EVELYN. No. *(A beat.)* You're my quietest child. You always have been. Sherry talks with every breath, but you never tell me anything, really, about yourself. Mrs. O'Connor saw you the other day.

KESS. Mrs. O'Connor?

EVELYN. You remember her. Your fourth-grade teacher? Always smiles and wears purple? Large teeth? Anyway, she said she still remembers you from then — just the way you were: stiff as a little post, quiet as could be.

KESS. I was not stiff.

EVELYN. Oh, yes you were. She remembers it. She said it was just like you were dead, only you could move from place to place. Isn't that an odd way to put it? I can see what she means, though. Do you have a move? What are you doing?

KESS. *(Having begun to cry silently.)* Nothing.

EVELYN. Are you crying?

KESS. No, I'm fine.

EVELYN. You are. You're crying and you're not making a sound. How do you do that? Cry silently like that. You always cry that way.

KESS. I do not cry silently! I cry out loud like everyone else.

EVELYN. Such a quiet one.

KESS. I was not quiet. You just couldn't hear me.

EVELYN. You were out of the house before I even knew you were that way. "Gay," I mean. Did you know? Back then?

KESS. Of course.

EVELYN. Really? How early?

KESS. Always. There wasn't much I could do about it around here.

EVELYN. Well, of course not. I should hope not.

KESS. There were some things. The woods, for example.

EVELYN. The woods?

KESS. When you were like me, the woods were the only place you could... (*Evelyn suddenly rises.*)

EVELYN. I have to use the bathroom, dear. You go on talking if you want. (*She exits for the bathroom.*)

KESS. (*As she goes.*) Hey, you asked me. I'm willing to tell you. I will tell you. Mom... (*But Evelyn is gone. Kess waits a beat, then goes on in a loud voice.*) I hated the woods. I hated the birds and trees and spiders and ... ticks. But when you're sixteen, and you want a lover — and it has to be a girl or you wouldn't be in love — you have to become a YWCA counselor and go to the woods. And just hope some other YWCA counselor is there for the same reason. And pray that people don't find out about you and fire you because they think you want to sleep with eight-year-old campers or something. I spent three summers lying terrified in a puptent for one affair that lasted two weeks, with a counselor I didn't even like. (*A beat.*) Mom? I know you can hear me.

EVELYN. (*Off.*) Go ahead and play. I'll be right out. (*Kess picks up the board and pours the letters into the box. Evelyn reenters.*)

KESS. Hi.

EVELYN. Did you win?

KESS. It was a tie.

EVELYN. I don't know what happened. Nature just suddenly called, loud and clear. (*A beat.*) So. What'll we do now?

KESS. Whatever you like.

EVELYN. (*Her eyes suddenly lighting up.*) Let's bake!

KESS. Bake?

EVELYN. Sure. We'll make something fun, for when the girls get home.

KESS. It's getting late...

EVELYN. Oh, come on. Remember when we used to do that? On nights your father was ... when he was out? Jo'd be sleeping upstairs, and you and I would bake for hours together. Biscuits, rolls, cookies — whatever we liked. It would get so late, but you never wanted to stop. I'd say something about the time, and you'd just go, "Ssshhh," and we'd keep on baking.

KESS. Mom...

EVELYN. Or I'd say, "Let's wake up Jo and give her some," and you'd shake your head *no*. Very firmly. Remember how it was? Just the two of us, late at night, like the real bakers?

KESS. *(A beat.)* All right, let's bake.

EVELYN. Good! *(Moves toward the kitchen.)* I can't tell you what having you back has meant, Kess. You give me back my sense of control. *(Suddenly we hear Sherry and Jo outside the porch.)*

SHERRY. *(Off, drunkenly.)* Come on, Jo — can't you recognize your own house?

JO. *(Off, drunkenly.)* It looks different.

SHERRY. *(Helping her through the front door.)* Believe me, this is it. Hi. We're drunk.

KESS. Jo, you said you weren't going to drink.

JO. *(Collapsing on the couch.)* I didn't.

SHERRY. Relax. She only had two beers.

JO. Two and a half.

SHERRY. You shouldn't have had any. Maybe then you wouldn't've been such a social disaster.

JO. I was not a social disaster.

EVELYN. Jo, are you all right?

JO. I'm fine. Am I lying down?

EVELYN. *(To Sherry.)* What is wrong with her?

SHERRY. Nothing. She flopped, that's all.

EVELYN. Flopped?

JO. Sherry fixed me up. Do you believe it? My little sister fixed me up. With the bartender.

KESS. Sherry, what did you...?

SHERRY. He's a terrific guy. Really easy to work with. At least he was.

JO. He was so handsome. Wasn't he?

SHERRY. You blew it. You froze up every time he talked to you.

JO. I couldn't talk to a man that beautiful.

SHERRY. You wasted two hours of his time. He was really trying. I never saw him work so hard. He liked you, stupid. *(To the others.)* She was just sitting there like Helen Keller all through it. Finally he says, "Look — I've asked you 50 questions. How about one

101

answer?" Know what she says? "I'm pregnant." She told him she was pregnant.

JO. He asked what I did.

SHERRY. Bartenders are not looking for pregnant women. It's a well-known fact. They don't find them attractive.

JO. I thought I had a special glow.

SHERRY. Yeah, well you glowed him right out of your life. Why do you put all that on somebody when all you want is to get laid?

JO. I did not want to get laid.

SHERRY. There's nothing wrong with it. Some people even like it. *(Suddenly Evelyn throws the* Scrabble *game to the floor. The letters scatter. They look at her. She smiles sweetly, with genuine embarrassment.)*

EVELYN. I'm getting a little tired. Maybe I'd better go to bed.

KESS. Mom, no ... you don't have to...

EVELYN. That's all right.

JO. I wasn't really trying to get ... you know.

EVELYN. I know. That's all right. Good night.

KESS. We were going to bake...

EVELYN. Another time. *(To Sherry.)* I'm glad you got her home alive. *(Evelyn exits to the stairs.)*

KESS. Good going.

SHERRY. I didn't throw it.

KESS. *(To Jo.)* You too.

JO. I'm pregnant and I'm proud. *(Kess starts picking up the* Scrabble *game.)*

SHERRY. You're pregnant and you're dateless. God, look at us. It's 10:30 and we're home.

KESS. Sherry, help me with this.

SHERRY. Are you kidding? Get Mom to.

JO. *(Rolling off the couch, onto the floor.)* I'll help.

SHERRY. *(Watching them.)* I can't believe it. This is what I get? After three nights of intense therapy?

KESS. Therapy? You've been taking her out to bars.

102

SHERRY. I've been introducing her to alternative lifestyles. She's the one who wanted to go.

JO. I just want to forget about Don.

KESS. There are better ways.

SHERRY. No, there aren't. Meet new guys. It's the code I live by.

KESS. Yeah, right.

JO. He really was good-looking.

KESS. Wonderful.

SHERRY. What are you mad about? Jo enjoyed herself tonight. She didn't walk around all mopey like she does here.

KESS. How does it feel to be eternally thirteen?

SHERRY. Great. And I'll tell you what else feels great. Getting Jo out of this house and away from a crazy woman.

KESS. *Mom is not a crazy woman.*

SHERRY. She isn't? You don't think it's crazy, trying to kill yourself with a dinner set?

KESS. You heard Dr. Hanson the same as I did. The same as all of us did.

SHERRY. You think I believe a man who's only seen her once?

KESS. He works with her out there.

SHERRY. But he only looked at her once! Yesterday. And I'm supposed to believe him when he says, "Oh, her behavior's just a little extreme — she's not really deeply emotionally disturbed?"

KESS. Yes!

SHERRY. Well, I think it's bullshit. He just doesn't want to be near her, either.

KESS. *(A beat.)* He said, if you'll recall, that she doesn't need to be committed. She just needs to work out some problems here, with us. I think that could happen a lot faster if you guys would stop going out every night.

SHERRY. What do you think we should do? Sit around and have tea all day?

KESS. It might help.

SHERRY. Wonderful. We have tea for a week, and then you

leave for Minnesota again.

KESS. Who says I'm leaving in a week?

SHERRY. You have to go back sometime. Face it, Kess, you can't do her any good.

KESS. What good are you doing her?

SHERRY. *I'm* ignoring her. *(A beat.)* Who did you come down here for, anyway? I thought it was Jo.

KESS. *(Tiredly.)* Everybody. I came down for everybody.

SHERRY. I think you came down for you. *(A beat.)* To hell with this, I'm going to dance. *(Sherry moves toward her room.)*

JO. Oh ... Sherry, *no...*

SHERRY. *(Disappearing into her room.)* Why not? Time for music!

JO. You always play it too loud...

SHERRY. *(Off.)* Too loud? You're crazy! *(Loud rock music suddenly issues forth. Sherry reenters, as Kess exits into the kitchen.)*

JO. This is not considerate!

SHERRY. *(Dancing.)* Why? 'Cause it's what I like?

JO. You do this all the time! *(As they speak, Kess reenters, carrying a pair of scissors, such that Sherry doesn't see them. Kess goes into Sherry's room. The music stops.)*

SHERRY. Hey! Turn that back on! *(Kess returns, with the scissors.)* What are you doing?

KESS. *(Working the scissors.)* You need new speaker wires.

SHERRY. *What?!* *(She hurries into her room. Kess looks at Jo on her way upstairs.)*

KESS. I'll expect everybody for tea at 5 tomorrow.

JO. Kess... *(But Kess disappears upstairs.)*

SHERRY. *(Off.)* You're a *barbarian!* *(Reentering.)* Where is she?

JO. She went up...

SHERRY. *(Starting for the stairs.)* I'll kill her!

JO. *(Grabbing her.)* Sherry, stop...!

SHERRY. You screwed-up, over-achieving dyke!

JO. *(Holding her.)* Sherry...

SHERRY. *I'm gonna rip up all your books!*

JO. Sherry, let's do something fun, ok?
SHERRY. *I'm gonna blow up your car!*
JO. Sherry...!
SHERRY. *You hear me!?*
JO. Let's do something fun! Please? Let's just do something fun!
*(Lights fade quickly to black.)*

# Scene Two

*Friday afternoon, the next day. Kess and Evelyn enter from the
kitchen. Kess carries tea for four on a tray, which she sets on a
low table near the couch.*

KESS. *(In a loud voice, as she enters.)* Come on, everybody. This is
going to be fun.
EVELYN. Where should I sit?
KESS. Anywhere. Wherever you're comfortable. *(Evelyn looks
dubiously at all potential seats. Kess points out a chair.)* How
about there?
EVELYN. *(Sitting.)* All right.
KESS. Sherry? Jo? You coming?
SHERRY. *(Off, in the kitchen.)* We're thinking about it.
KESS. Come on, come on — the tea'll get cold. *(To Evelyn.)* You
want cream, right?
EVELYN. Thanks.
KESS. *(Sing-song.)* Sher-ry, Jo-o...
SHERRY. *(Entering in a dirty shirt and jeans, mimicking Kess's
tone.)* All ri-ight, we're com-ing.
JO. *(Entering, neatly dressed.)* Where do you want us to sit?
KESS. Wherever you like. *(Sherry and Jo look around dubiously.
Kess points out two places.)* Ok, you: there. You: there. *(They sit.)*
Everyone comfortable? How do you want your tea?
SHERRY. In my room.

KESS. Jo?

JO. Just plain.

KESS. *(Handing a cup to Jo, then Sherry.)* Fine. Sherry? *(Sherry pauses, then takes a cup.)* Good. Now. Here we are — just as Dr. Hanson suggested — all four of us, sitting down together. First, I want to thank you all for agreeing to try.

SHERRY. I'm only doing it to show I can. Besides, I'm tired of working on my sculpture.

KESS. That's ok. Dr. Hanson said it's more important to go through the motions of being a happy family than it is to actually feel like one — at least, at this point. The more we act like a normal, happy family, the better the chance we'll become one someday. The new way of behaving will become as natural and unavoidable as the old, bad way.

SHERRY. I like the old bad way.

KESS. I know. But for now, let's act nice. Ok? As an experiment. So — who'd like to be the first to say something nice? *(A long silence.)*

EVELYN. The tea is very good.

KESS. Thank you. That's a good start. Would anyone else like to offer something positive? *(Another awkward silence.)*

JO. I like my cup. I mean, I've always liked these cups, ever since you got them.

EVELYN. Thank you.

KESS. Good. Anyone else? *(A beat.)* Sherry, I think I'm getting to like your sculpture.

SHERRY. Fuck you.

JO. *Sherry...*

SHERRY. I didn't raise my voice.

KESS. That's not the point.

SHERRY. Well, you're only saying that. You don't like my stuff any more than anyone else.

KESS. I know, but I'm pretending to.

SHERRY. Then you're just lying.

KESS. That's right.

SHERRY. Why?

KESS. *To be nice!! (With more control.)* Sorry. Please — just say thank you, ok? You don't have to know what it means; you don't have to feel it. Just say it. *(A beat. Sherry rises.)*

SHERRY. No way.

JO. Why not?

SHERRY. *(Moving towards her room.)* This is stupid. I don't want to do this.

KESS. You mean, you can't do it.

SHERRY. *(Stopping by her door.)* I can do it.

KESS. No, you can't.

SHERRY. I can.

KESS. Prove it.

SHERRY. *(A beat. With extreme unpleasantness.)* Thank you, Kess. That was a lovely compliment about my sculpture.

KESS. You're welcome. Wouldn't you like to come sit down again?

SHERRY. I'll stand.

KESS. That's fine with me — everybody else?

JO. Sure.

EVELYN. Sherry can do what she likes. She always does.

SHERRY. You call that positive?!

KESS. Mom, I thought we agreed to try this.

EVELYN. Aren't I doing it right?

KESS. Let's start over. How about if each of us talks about something she's doing, and then the rest of us find a positive comment to make about it? How would that be?

SHERRY. Stupid.

KESS. Sherry, why don't you tell about your sculpture? What do you like about it most?

SHERRY. It's grotesque.

KESS. *(Forging ahead.)* Ok. Grotesque. Good. Why do you like that?

SHERRY. It scares Mrs. Anderberg. Ever since I put the little fawn and the stable boy together in an unnatural act. Makes her weed her garden a lot faster.

KESS. Does anyone have anything ... positive to say about that?

JO. Well ... weeding faster is probably good exercise.

KESS. Good, Jo. That's a positive comment. So, fine. So. We have one ... sort of ... civil exchange. Let's try for more. Mom? Tell us what you've been doing.

EVELYN. Me? Oh — nothing. You know me.

KESS. What'd you do this morning?

EVELYN. Went out for a walk.

KESS. And?

EVELYN. I walked.

KESS. Did you see anybody?

EVELYN. Certainly.

KESS. *(A beat.)* Who?

EVELYN. Who? Um ... Mrs. Matthews.

KESS. How was she?

EVELYN. Fine. I didn't really have a very eventful morning. Why don't we go to Jo?

KESS. Did you and Mrs. Matthews talk?

EVELYN. Yes, but...

KESS. What about?

EVELYN. Oh, nothing much.

KESS. What?

EVELYN. Just ... Jo.

KESS. Jo. Fine. Did she have anything nice to say about Jo?

EVELYN. Of course. She's always liked Jo. Why don't we talk about...?

KESS. What exactly did she say about Jo?

EVELYN. Nothing. Just that Jo's a very strong girl in some ways.

KESS. Did you hear that, Jo? Now, that's exactly what I mean, Mom. Why should you be slow to tell us a thing like that?

EVELYN. Well...

KESS. What's strong about her? How did it come up?

EVELYN. Oh, I don't know...

KESS. It must've come from something.

EVELYN. Not really.

KESS. Mom, what aren't you telling us?

EVEI.YN. Nothing.

JO. Mom? What is it?

EVELYN. Oh, Jo — I'll tell you later, all right? When we're alone.

JO. Is it private?

EVELYN. Well...

SHERRY. So what is it? Don getting married or something?

EVELYN. Who told you?

SHERRY. You're kidding. That was a joke.

JO. Don's getting married?

KESS. Mom, what are you...?

JO. Who to?

EVELYN. I was going to tell you later...

JO. *Who to?!*

EVELYN. Heidi Joy Duckly. Mrs. Matthews heard it this morning from Heidi's mother.

JO. Oh, God...

KESS. Jo...

JO. Oh, *God.*

KESS. Jo, listen — there are two ways to handle this.

SHERRY. Yeah? Suicide and what?

KESS. Shut up!

SHERRY. Very positive.

KESS. Jo, we can fly off the handle here, or we can be calm about it. We can find something useful in it.

JO. *Useful?!*

KESS. Yes. Something. That's the problem with us. Trouble comes, and we break down. Let's not do that.

SHERRY. Heidi's folks must feel great to get rid of her. The wedding oughta be a prize pork show.

KESS. *Sherry.*

SHERRY. She's only losing a Subaru.

EVELYN. I think you're lucky to be rid of him.

JO. I'm not *lucky! (She rises, moves toward the stairs.)*

KESS. Where are you going?

JO. My room! *(But she stops suddenly, slumps against the archway.)*

SHERRY. What are you stopping for?

JO. We used to make love up there.

EVELYN. That's the trouble with an old house. It always fills up with ghosts. Good memories turn into bad ones. I know I see your father in every room. Not literally, of course. Speaking of memories, Jo — do you know what I've been doing in the attic?

JO. What?

EVELYN. I've been painting. Just a little, every day. Guess what I've been painting.

JO. What?

EVELYN. The baby furniture. All the baby furniture — yours and Kess's and Sherry's. I've been making it new for your new baby. I was going to keep it a secret, but I think you can use a little good news right now. Would you like to come up and see?

JO. Well...

EVELYN. Oh, come on. It's turning out so nice. Your baby is going to live right here with us — with her mother and her grandma. Just the way I did when I was a little girl. And she's going to be every bit as happy and well-cared-for and loved as I was. Doesn't that sound nice? Wouldn't you like to come up and see?

JO. All right.

KESS. Jo...

EVELYN. *(Rising.)* Good.

KESS. *Jo* — don't you think it would be better to keep trying this? You can see the furniture later.

JO. *(A beat.)* I'm going up. *(Jo turns and hurries upstairs.)*

KESS. Jo...!

EVELYN. Kess, I'm sorry this game didn't work out. Maybe we'll do better another time. *(Evelyn exits upstairs.)*

KESS. *(A beat.)* You see what I'm trying to do, don't you?

SHERRY. Sure. You're trying to make a family where there isn't one. *(A beat.)* Jo and I are going to see the new James Bond tonight. Want to come? *(A beat.)* Be a chance to get away from Mom.

KESS. *(A beat.)* All right.

SHERRY. Good. *(Sherry exits into her room. Kess sighs, leans her head back on the couch. Her hand moves up to touch the cameo. Lights slowly fade to black.)*

# Scene Three

*Late that same night. The room is empty, the tea set is gone. After a moment, we hear the giggling of Kess, Jo and Sherry outside the porch.*

SHERRY. *(Off.)* I'm not going in first. Jo, you go.

JO. *(Off.)* Why don't you?

SHERRY. *(Off.)* Kess?

KESS. *(Off.)* You're standing next to the door. Go on in.

SHERRY. *(Off.)* What if Mom's in there?

KESS. *(Off.)* Of course she's in there...

SHERRY. *(Off.)* But what if she's waiting for us? With a plate?

KESS and JO. *(Off, disapprovingly.)* Sherry...

SHERRY. *(Entering.)* Ok, ok. Lousy joke.

JO. *(Entering with Kess.)* Very lousy.

KESS. Mom? We're back. Mom? *(Looking into the kitchen.)* Where are you?

JO. I'll go look in her room. *(Jo exits upstairs.)*

KESS. You think we made enough noise walking home?

SHERRY. I still say we should've hit Popeye's for a beer.

KESS. Jo's pregnant.

SHERRY. *I'm* not.

KESS. It's been a long time since I actually enjoyed walking around this town. Maybe I should make some coffee.

SHERRY. What is this thing between you and caffeine? *(Jo reenters.)*

JO. She's ok.

SHERRY. She's ok and I'm sober. *(Flops into a chair.)*
KESS. I'm glad we did this tonight. We saw a good movie.
JO. You think so? I didn't like it.
SHERRY. You're just mad 'cause the woman didn't die.
JO. I think that really changes things...
SHERRY. Sure. Dead, you don't mind. What you hate is when they sail off into the sunset for a lifetime of meaningless sex.
JO. Well, yes, as a matter of fact.
SHERRY. Believe me, big sister — it's the best way to get out of this house. Dedicate yourself to meaningless sex.
JO. Don't be ridiculous.
SHERRY. I mean it. You should go out and do it with whoever you want, whenever you feel like it, and not think about it afterwards. Puts you in a very different state of mind.
JO. I can't do that.
SHERRY. Sure you can. Want me to set you up? I know a bunch of guys — we'll toss their names in a hat. It's what I do myself.
KESS. How many lovers have you had?
SHERRY. My share. And all meaningless, too. I'm the first lady of meaningless sex. You guys screw up 'cause you think it's supposed to mean something.
JO. It does.
SHERRY. No, it doesn't. I slept with a guy once 'cause I liked his socks. What'd that mean?
KESS. Not much, I guess.
SHERRY. Damn right. I've slept with guys who would make you vomit. This one I knew was really sloppy. A total pig. But I wondered if maybe he was just profound and didn't have time for cleaning. So I went home with him.
KESS. Naturally.
SHERRY. His place was incredible. It looked like he cooked in the bedroom and slept in the kitchen. So anyway — we did it on this bare mattress on the floor. And when we got done, he rolled over, reached under the dresser, among all the hairballs and shit, and pulled out a spoon.

JO. Oh, God! God! Stop it!

SHERRY. And he said, "Want some chili?"

JO. Sherry, stop it! Ew!

SHERRY. Hey — truth is gross.

JO. Well, I've never had any meaningless sex.

SHERRY. Ever faked an orgasm?

KESS. I faked an orgasm with a woman. *(They look at her.)* I mean, if you want to talk meaningless.

SHERRY. You're kidding.

KESS. If you want to talk true meaningless, I've had sex with a man, just so I could meet his sister. Top that.

SHERRY. You really did that?

KESS. Yes, when I was young and stupid.

SHERRY. I had sex with a guy at a concert and never even knew his name. Top that.

JO. You guys...

KESS. I had sex with a woman in a dorm laundry, and never even saw her face.

SHERRY. Yeah, but did you talk to her? I never talked to my guy at the concert.

JO. You guys! Is this all we can talk about? I don't care what either of you did. I think it's more disgusting to talk about that kind of sex than to have it.

SHERRY. I'd rather be disgusting than pitiful. You've got the most screwed-up sex life I ever...

JO. *I'm* screwed? You're the one who always forgets who she had the night before.

SHERRY. At least I have someone to forget.

JO. I had someone.

SHERRY. Yeah, and now he's marrying Heidi. Hope you and Mom'll be very happy together.

JO. *(A beat. Quietly.)* Well, at least with Don it wasn't meaningless.

SHERRY. Oh, yes it was.

KESS. Why don't we talk about the movie?

SHERRY. It was. Simpleton thinks Don was faithful the whole

time they were together.

JO. He was faithful.

SHERRY. Don slept with at least six girls while you were dating. Including Heidi.

JO. How do you know that?

SHERRY. They told me.

JO. You're lying! That's just a complete lie.

SHERRY. Wake up. Don sleeps with everybody in town.

KESS. You guys...

JO. He does not!

SHERRY. Oh yeah? He slept with me! *(A beat. They are all perfectly still.)* Once.

JO. When? *(A beat.)* When?!

SHERRY. After you dropped him. What do you care? It's all meaningless.

JO. Not to me!

SHERRY. For God's sake, Heidi's the one who should be mad, not you. I wouldn't't've told you, but you just keep being so pitiful about it all. You want him and then you don't want him... *(She trails off, in deep embarrassment.)* I'm sorry.

JO. It's so easy for us to criticize Mom. To say she made us like we are. But she never did anything just for the cruelty of it. If she hurts us, it's because she's afraid, and disappointed and doesn't want to be left alone. But we do it just for the fun.

KESS. Jo...

JO. We're supposed to be the healthy ones. Aren't we? Aren't we? *(She rises.)* Good night. *(Jo exits in silence. Kess looks at Sherry.)*

SHERRY. I'm sorry. It slipped out. *(A beat.)* Maybe we should have some coffee.

KESS. As long as you make it on your knees.

SHERRY. *(Exiting into the kitchen.)* I said I was sorry. *(Kess starts for the stairs, stops. Sherry calls from the kitchen.)* Hey, what are these letters on the counter?

KESS. The mail. I brought it in today.

SHERRY. *(Off.)* No wonder I can never find it. *(A beat.)* Hey! Hey, Kess! I got a letter! From Spinner!

114

KESS. Spinner?

SHERRY. *(Off.)* My biker!

KESS. Oh. Wonderful.

SHERRY. *(Reentering with the letter.)* No, Kess — wait! It's from a *gallery!!* He enclosed a letter from a gallery! It's the ... um, the Raoul Gallery in ... um, *BROOKLYN!!* They want to talk to *me!*

KESS. About what?

SHERRY. About me, about my work! Don't you see? Spinner really took my stuff to New York! I didn't think he would, but he did! And they love my slides! They're calling my stuff a whole new school of art! It's ... it's ... um, Post-Post-Modern Infantilist! Isn't that great!? I'm knocking 'em dead back there!

KESS. Sherry...

SHERRY. Kess! They want to do a show! They want me there right now! Just when I was starting to think he didn't really work for Walt Disney!

KESS. They want you where?

SHERRY. New York! For the show. They want to fly me in. Do you know how they live in New York? They are total animals! I can't *wait!* I'm flying tomorrow.

KESS. Who pays?

SHERRY. What?

KESS. Who buys the plane ticket?

SHERRY. I do. Why not? The whole point is getting the chance.

KESS. What's the name of the gallery?

SHERRY. The Raoul Gallery.

KESS. Sherry.

SHERRY. What?

KESS. The *Raoul* Gallery? In Brooklyn?

SHERRY. What's wrong with that?

KESS. It's ridiculous. It's a joke.

SHERRY. You think they're not real?

KESS. Sherry...

SHERRY. *(Defensively.)* They're real. They've got a letterhead. They're real.

KESS. Sure.

SHERRY. They're real!

KESS. Can't you see that Spinner is just doing this to you? God knows why, but...

SHERRY. Spinner is a professional!

KESS. A professional what — that's the question.

SHERRY. Spinner and I had the one honest exchange of my whole senior year.

KESS. How much did you exchange?

SHERRY. Damn it, if he says it's real, then it's real!

KESS. Sherry, look at me. Come on, look in my face. Do you really believe there is a Post-Post-Modern Infantilist school of art?

SHERRY. *(Exploding.) Yes!!* God damn it! I believe more in that than in this goddamn, stupid fucking family! There *is* a Raoul Gallery!

KESS. Sherry...

SHERRY. There is!

KESS. Sherry, take it easy...

SHERRY. I'm having a show! And I'm going!

KESS. *(Touching her.)* Shh — I know you are.

SHERRY. I am!

KESS. I know, it's all right.

SHERRY. It's in Brooklyn! *(She is near tears.)*

KESS. *(Taking hold of her.)* I know. I know it is.

SHERRY. Brooklyn, New York. And I'm going, I'm...

KESS. Shh. I know. You're going to New York. I know. You're going to New York. *(They are silent. Kess holds her and rocks her.)*

SHERRY. *(Quietly.)* How did Mom live a whole life here?

KESS. She had us. *(Lights slowly fade to black.)*

# Scene Four

*Afternoon, the next day. No one is onstage. Jo rushes in the front door.*

JO. Kess? Kess!?

KESS. *(Off.)* I'm upstairs!

JO. Can you come down?

KESS. *(Off.)* In a minute. *(Jo looks around the room, goes to Sherry's door, looks in.)*

JO. Sherry? You home? *(No response. Jo stands nervously.)* Kess!

KESS. *(Off.)* I'm coming, I'm coming! *(Kess enters from upstairs.)* What's wrong?

JO. Where were you?

KESS. Upstairs.

JO. Nobody seemed to be here.

KESS. What's wrong?

JO. Where's Mom?

KESS. She's at the store.

JO. Where's Sherry?

KESS. With Mom. Jo, what are you...?

JO. So, they're not here.

KESS. *(A beat.)* Jo, where have you been all morning?

JO. On an errand.

KESS. A four-hour errand?

JO. I had to go over to Waterloo. *(A beat.)* Kess, do you remember when you asked me to come up and stay with you?

KESS. Yes.

JO. Did you mean that?

KESS. Well ... yes, at the time...

JO. I want to come up. I want to come up right now.

KESS. Now?

117

JO. Yes. And I want to stay. I want to stay for the summer at least, maybe a lot longer.

KESS. Jo, what are you talking about?

JO. I want to come up. You said I could come up. You said that roommate of yours, that...

KESS. Susan.

JO. You said Susan thinks it's ok.

KESS. Well, yes, but ... why now?

JO. I have to get away from Mom.

KESS. What'd she do?

JO. Nothing.

KESS. *(A beat.)* Yesterday you and Mom were planning which room to use for the nursery. What happened? Why are you so scared?

JO. I just did a ... very odd thing. I went over to Heidi's house. I thought I was only going over to talk with her. Just to ... look her in the eye once, and ask her if she really slept with Don while he and I were ... you know, like Sherry said...

KESS. I know.

JO. But as I turned the corner I saw her pull out and drive away. So I followed her.

KESS. To Waterloo? *(Jo nods.)* What did you do there?

JO. I watched. I watched the way she drove. I watched the way she shopped. She hit all the bridal shops, plus a few others. She's a good shopper.

KESS. Did she see you?

JO. No. I hid. I stayed two cars behind her, like on tv, and I hid behind pillars in the stores. I never lost her. I stared at her and stared at her for four hours, and she never saw me and I never lost her. I didn't want to talk with her anymore. I just wanted to watch her. On the way home, I thought, "My God, why am I doing this!?" But I just kept following. I thought, "*Mom* should be driving this car. I should be Mom doing this." Then I thought, "I am." Kess, I love Mom.

KESS. I know that.

JO. I thought of how I'll be in ten years, if I stay with Mom. Kess, I can't be Mom. How can I help her if I'm just like her?

KESS. Jo...

JO. I want to leave tomorrow. And I want to stay with you. Is that all right?

KESS. Well ... I'm not sure that's the best idea anymore.

JO. *Kess...*

KESS. Jo, we can't leave Mom the way she is. I thought we could, but that was before I saw how lonely she was...

JO. I don't care...

KESS. Besides, she could hurt herself. That's why I've stayed down here so long — to make sure she's all right.

JO. She's all right; let's go.

KESS. She's not all right.

JO. She never will be!

KESS. Jo, what if I stay down here another few days, and then come back on regular visits, once a month, for as long as ... for as long as it takes? Could you stay here then?

JO. No! I'm coming up north, and I'm living with you. You offered it. And I need it.

KESS. Jo...

JO. You owe me! *(A beat.)* I don't care how guilty you feel, Kess. I don't. We can't save Mom. Save me. *(We suddenly hear Sherry and Evelyn at the front door.)*

SHERRY. Here we are — Shopper's Anonymous. *(Entering.)* Hi, everybody. It's everybody else. Where'd you go this morning, Jo? Somewhere fun?

JO. No.

SHERRY. *(Carrying the bag into the kitchen.)* Should've come with us. The store was full of living sculptures.

EVELYN. *(At the screen door, with a bag of groceries.)* Can someone help me with the door?

KESS. *(Hurrying to open it.)* Oh — sorry.

EVELYN. Thank you. Hi, Jo. Did you have a good morning? Oh, let me set these *down. (Doing so, on the couch.)* There. Why is modern food so heavy? Sherry and I decided to have a big dinner tonight, for Kess. We haven't really done that yet, and Kess is

119

starting to fit in so well.

SHERRY. *(Reentering, to Kess.)* Yeah. Are you sure you're not crazy?

EVELYN. Jo, do you want to help me cook it?

JO. No.

EVELYN. Oh? Are you busy tonight?

JO. No.

EVELYN. *(A beat.)* Oh. Well, maybe you can, Kess.

JO. She can't either.

EVELYN. Why not?

KESS. Jo, this isn't the right time...

JO. She'll be packing. So will I.

EVELYN. Packing? What for?

JO. I'm going to Minneapolis with her.

EVELYN. *(A beat.)* Really?

JO. Yes.

EVELYN. I don't understand. You mean for a visit?

JO. No.

EVELYN. For longer?

JO. Forever.

EVELYN. *(A beat.)* You're pregnant. You can't travel.

JO. Two and a half months. We're not going by covered wagon.

KESS. Jo...

EVELYN. Oh, this is a joke. Isn't it? You and Kess have created a joke. Oh, I see now. Well, it's very funny. *(She takes an orange out of the bag.)* Isn't this a joke, Kess?

KESS. No, not exactly...

JO. Mom, I've been following Heidi around.

EVELYN. Following Heidi? What for?

JO. Just to watch her. Just to watch what she does all day.

SHERRY. That must be a thrill.

JO. I couldn't help myself. I just followed her.

EVELYN. We all have impulses that are hard to control. *(She tosses the orange casually onto the couch.)*

JO. I'm afraid I'll go crazy.

120

EVELYN. *(Flaring.)* What in hell do you know about it?! I've *been* in mental hospitals!

JO. I was only...

EVELYN. You were only trying to sneak out of here! In the dust of everybody else galloping away! *(She tosses another orange onto the couch.)*

SHERRY. Mom, what are you doing?

EVELYN. What?

SHERRY. You're putting oranges on the couch.

EVELYN. Well, of course I'm putting oranges on the couch! This is my house. People used to live in it. *(A beat.)* Who's going to stay here?

JO. Well ... Sherry...

EVELYN. She'll be out the door twenty seconds after commencement.

JO. Kess says she'll visit...

EVELYN. Who'll *live* here?

JO. When I followed Heidi, I even followed her home. I did. I sat in my car and watched her mother come out and help her bring in the things she'd bought. They were laughing. They looked like sisters.

EVELYN. Jo...

JO. You're crazy! And when you're not crazy, you're angry. When you're not angry, you're demanding. It can be months between times we have any pleasure!

EVELYN. Jo...

JO. I'm the only person who has ever put up with you!

EVELYN. *(Reaching to embrace her.)* Jo...

JO. *(Retreating.)* No! I'm living with Kess. I have to. I have to.

EVELYN. *(A beat.)* You can't. You can't, and that's all there is to it. It's a ridiculous idea. Kess, was this your idea?

KESS. No...

EVELYN. Jo could never live with you. She's going to have a baby.

KESS. What are you talking about?

EVELYN. You could never live with a baby.

121

KESS. Of course I could live with a baby.

EVELYN. You don't know the first thing. You'd panic in a minute.

KESS. I can live with a baby!

EVELYN. *You don't know what they want!*

JO. It's my baby!

EVELYN. You shut up! I'm talking to Kess.

KESS. Mom, what if Jo just comes up for a little while? Just to see how it goes?

JO. *No.*

KESS. We could come down on visits.

JO. *No!*

EVELYN. Do you really want to take her from me?

JO. I'm going!

KESS. I don't want to take anybody from anybody...

EVELYN. Well, that's what you're doing. You girls would like a world full of strangers, wouldn't you? You'd like it if there was no connection between people at all. *(Focussing on Jo.)* Well, there isn't. Not unless you make one. Kess and Henry taught me that. They were the two most silent people I ever knew. For eight years they were my whole family. Henry and Kess. Can you imagine what dinners were like? I had to beg Henry for you. You were all I ever got out of my whole family. You're the only one I can look at and not see Henry.

JO. *(Backing away.)* I can't help you.

EVELYN. Then who can?

JO. I can't help you.

EVELYN. I just need you to be here a little more. Just a few days.

JO. I can't! I can't help you, I can't be with you, I can't look at you, I can't think about you, I can't talk to you, I can't hope for you...

EVELYN. Can you love me?

JO. *It's not a matter of love!!*

EVELYN. Can you?

JO. Kess!

EVELYN. What do you think families are for? Do you think parents die when you turn 21? I might as well have, if all you're leaving me is the Mental Health Institute and a townful of people saying, "Poor Evelyn Briggs. First her husband walks off, then every one of her daughters abandons her."

KESS. We're not abandoning you. We'll be back. We'll visit.

EVELYN. When? How often?

KESS. Once a month.

EVELYN. Once a month?

KESS. Twice, then. Twice a month.

JO. No...!

KESS. *Jo!* Mom? What do you say?

EVELYN. I have wasted my life raising three *animals!!*

JO. *(To Kess.)* I won't come down!

EVELYN. I lived my life for you! My mother lived her life for me. That's what family means — each generation destroying itself willingly, for what comes after. Even if it's you! *(A silence. Kess slowly unpins the cameo from her dress.)*

KESS. *(Quietly.)* Jo and I are going to go upstairs and pack. We'll talk about visits later. *(Placing the cameo on a table next to Evelyn.)* I think you should keep this for awhile. *(A beat. Kess starts for the stairs.)* Come on, Jo. *(As Jo starts after her, Evelyn reaches into the grocery bag and pulls out a can. She raises it high in the air.)*

SHERRY. Mom! *(Evelyn smashes the can down on the cameo.)*

JO. *NO!*

KESS. Mom!

SHERRY. Jesus! *(A beat. The heirloom is in pieces.)*

JO. How could you do that? How could you do that?!

EVELYN. Because it was mine. *(Lights fade to black.)*

# Scene Five

*Morning, the next day. Before lights rise we hear Sherry's voice in the darkness. Lights slowly fade up midway through her song to reveal her sitting with Kess's ballad book open in her lap.*

SHERRY.
"'Tis down in yonder garden green,
Love where we used to walk,
The finest flower that e'er was seen
Is withered to a stalk.
*(She shifts from the traditional tune to a punk version.)*
The stalk is withered dry, my love
So will our hearts decay..."
*(Kess enters through the porch, and Sherry immediately snaps the book shut.)*
KESS. Is Jo ready? I've got all my stuff in the car.
SHERRY. *(Holding the book up.)* You don't have this.
KESS. *(Taking it.)* Oh — thanks. Jo upstairs?
SHERRY. Guess so.
KESS. What'll you do? When we're gone?
SHERRY. Graduate. Move out.
KESS. *(A beat.)* You're welcome to come and see us, if you ever...
SHERRY. *(Suddenly rising.)* Look, I'm going to go over to Ed Randall's for awhile. If Mom asks, tell her I'm there, ok?
KESS. Sure... Don't you want to say goodby to Jo?
SHERRY. No, that's ok.
KESS. Sherry?
SHERRY. What?
KESS. Glad I got to know you again.
SHERRY. Yeah, well... see you in four years. *(Sherry exits out the front. Kess looks around the room a little nervously, then calls.)*
KESS. Jo-o! I'm all set! *(Jo enters from upstairs with a pair of bags.)*
JO. Here I am.
KESS. Is that all your stuff?
JO. The rest is in the car.

KESS. Well ... then, um ... let's go, I guess.

JO. Could you take these out? I'd like to say goodby to Mom.

KESS. I already tried. It's not much use.

JO. Could you anyway? *(Kess shrugs, takes the bags.)*

KESS. I'll be in the car. *(Kess exits out the front.)*

JO. *(Calling upstairs.)* Mom?! I'm leaving! Mom? Could you come down? *(Jo waits uncomfortably for a moment.)* Mom?! *(She waits again. Finally she shakes her head and starts for the front door. Evelyn appears from upstairs.)* Oh — um, we're leaving now.

EVELYN. I know.

JO. I'm sorry I took so long to pack. *(A beat.)* I'm going to write, you know. Whether or not you write back. *(A beat.)* And ... I will visit, after awhile. If you'd like me to. *(A beat.)* I talked to Mrs. Anderberg. She said she'll be glad to come over, as much as you need.

EVELYN. That's nice. She wasn't really born here, you know. She's from Michigan.

JO. I called Dr. Hanson. He'd like to talk with you sometime. Just talk. Whenever you'd like to.

EVELYN. *(A beat.)* Is there anything else?

JO. I want to hug you.

EVELYN. *(A beat.)* Go ahead. Hug me. *(Jo hesitates, then does so. Evelyn doesn't resist, but neither does she raise her arms to hug back. Jo steps back and stares at her.)*

JO. I could call when we get up there. This afternoon, I mean. *(A beat.)* I think I will. *(A beat. Jo starts to leave, stops.)* Should I? *(A beat. Jo leaves. Lights slowly fade to black as Evelyn remains still.)*

### THE END

# RICHES

*A Play in Three Scenes*

*For Jeanne*

*Riches,* as *War of the Roses,* was given its professional premiere at the Actors Theatre of Louisville as part of the Ninth Annual Humana Festival of New American Plays from February 19 through March 30, 1985. It was directed by Bill Partlan.

*Riches* was originally presented as a staged reading at the 1984 National Playwrights Conference at the Eugene O'Neill Memorial Theater Center.

## AUTHOR'S NOTE

The events of this play are fictional. The setting is not. The St. James Hotel, as described, does exist in Red Wing. It is a pleasant place to stay.

# CHARACTERS

DAVID RICH . . . . . . . 45, an advertising account executive

CAROLYN RICH . . . . . . . . . . . . . . . . . . . . . 41, his wife

# TIME

The present, a night in early September

# PLACE

The St. James Hotel, Red Wing, Minnesota

*Lights rise to reveal a third-floor corner room in the St. James Hotel of Red Wing, Minnesota. This is a century-old, restored brick structure. It's been decorated with that in mind: simple, elegant, American. A large bed on one side of the room, an impressive antique reproduction armoire against another. Windows on two walls. A small writing desk and chair is set in one corner, facing into the room. A vanity between the bed and the door to the bathroom. A night table on the other side of the bed, with a phone and hardcover book lying on it. At least one straight chair. David's jacket is draped over it. A door to the hall.*

*David lies on the bed, fully dressed in a suit and stocking feet.*

DAVID. Hey! You about ready?
CAROLYN. (*In the bathroom.*) Just about.
DAVID. Getting a little boring out here. There's no tv.
CAROLYN. (*Off.*) Read the book. That's why we brought it.
(*He rises, goes to the vanity, takes change, keys, etc. and puts them in his pocket. Suddenly he checks to see bathroom door is closed, goes to the armoire, opens it and gets a small box out of his suitbag. He puts the box in his jacket on the chair. He goes to a window, looks out. Takes out a handkerchief and blows his nose — a big blow, then three little ones. He picks up the book.*)
DAVID. I don't like reading books that we're both reading. Which place is mine?
CAROLYN. (*Off.*) The second one. I think. (*He looks at the cover, reads the title to himself.*)
DAVID. "The Art Of Friendship." Why are we reading the same book?
CAROLYN. (*Off.*) We like it. (*He sighs, closes the book.*) Are you ready to go?
DAVID. Um-hmm.
CAROLYN. (*Off.*) What'd you say?

DAVID. Yes. I am. (*A beat.*) Wish we could've gotten our old room back.

CAROLYN. (*Off.*) What?

DAVID. Our old room. For tonight. I wanted to sleep on the same bed we had on our honeymoon.

CAROLYN. (*Off.*) Oh. Right. (*She enters, putting on a shoe.*) This room isn't so bad. Practically identical. Just one floor down.

DAVID. Not the same, though. Not the very same.

CAROLYN. It's close enough.

DAVID. It's different. The view's a little different. You remember our honeymoon? (*He slips on his shoes.*)

CAROLYN. Why yes, I believe I do.

DAVID. Remember how you sat?

CAROLYN. How I sat?

DAVID. Yeah. On the corner of the bed. Remember?

CAROLYN. No . . .

DAVID. Sure you do. You made a big deal of it.

CAROLYN. It was a long time ago.

DAVID. It was our honeymoon. You remember. (*Moving her to a sitting position on the bed.*) Here. You sat just like this. Right there. On the corner. Cross your legs.

CAROLYN. (*Doing so.*) Honey, we're going to dinner.

DAVID. In a minute. (*Regards her.*) God. Just like it was yesterday. You walked into this room . . .

CAROLYN. Not this room.

DAVID. You took one look around, you . . . sat down on the corner of the bed and looked right up into my eyes. And you smiled. Smile.

CAROLYN. What?

DAVID. Go on. Give me a smile.

CAROLYN. (*Starting to rise.*) We should call Tom and Deb . . .

DAVID. (*Stopping her.*) No, come on. Smile. I'm remembering. (*She makes a dopey smile.*) No, no, no — come on. (*She smiles prettily.*) Oh, yeah. That's it. That's a lovely smile. Just like that.

CAROLYN. (*Starts to rise.*) Well, good . . .

DAVID. Sit down.

CAROLYN. I thought you were done.

DAVID. I'm not. (*She sits again.*) There was light coming in then, too. Just like now. You knew it. You knew exactly what you were doing. Sitting there right in front of a window, with the day's last light just . . . pouring all over you.

CAROLYN. (*Rising.*) What a nice memory.

DAVID. Sit down. Please?

CAROLYN. I sat down.

DAVID. No — keep sitting.

CAROLYN. I did keep sitting.

DAVID. Sit a little longer.

CAROLYN. I didn't want to sit any longer . . .

DAVID. Sit. (*Slowly, she sits.*) You sat still. For a very long time. Staring up into my eyes. You were a virgin.

CAROLYN. Yes, but now I'm hungry, so . . . (*She starts to rise.*)

DAVID. *Carolyn.* It's our anniversary. For God's sake, don't you want to be sentimental? (*She takes a beat, then completes the process of standing up.*)

CAROLYN. We should get to dinner.

DAVID. (*As she moves toward the vanity.*) What's so important about dinner?

CAROLYN. Tom and Deb'll be expecting us. Aren't you hungry?

DAVID. Well yes, but . . .

CAROLYN. Then let's eat. We have the whole weekend to feel sentimental. Really, it was a very nice memory. (*She kisses him on the cheek.*) So — I'll call and see if they're ready. Ok?

DAVID. Sure. Fine. I'll go pee.

CAROLYN. Ok. (*He exits into the bathroom as she dials.*) Tom? Hi. David and I are just about set for dinner here, and . . . What? Oh? Oh. Well — no, not at all. We're just sitting around. We can wait. How long will she be? Oh. (*She gives an irritated look, remains pleasant on the phone.*) You want us to meet you down in the restaurant, then? Ok. No, no. No problem. See you then. (*She hangs up. David reenters.*)

DAVID. They ready?

CAROLYN. Debby's still in the shower.

DAVID. How come?

CAROLYN. Judging by the happy sound in Tom's voice, I think they just got done.

DAVID. Oh. Well, she is cute.

CAROLYN. Everybody's cute at 20.

DAVID. How long they going to be?

CAROLYN. An hour.

DAVID. An hour?

CAROLYN. She has to do her hair.

DAVID. My God, she acts like a kid.

CAROLYN. She is a kid.

DAVID. Well, what the hell are *we* going to do?

CAROLYN. We could go down to the bar.

DAVID. For an hour? How much do you want to drink?

CAROLYN. We could nurse one.

DAVID. It'd be more like intensive care. An hour. My God. (*He looks around for a moment, goes to the window, looks out. She picks up the book, sits on the bed and starts to read. He looks around after a moment, moves to the bed, slips off his shoes, sits next to her. She looks up; he smiles.*)

CAROLYN. No.

DAVID. Why not? We've got an hour.

CAROLYN. I'm all dressed.

DAVID. So am I.

CAROLYN. I don't feel like revenge sex.

DAVID. Revenge?

CAROLYN. They-made-us-late-now-let's-make-them-late. I don't enjoy that.

DAVID. Why not? It's a game. Tom and I have been playing it for years.

CAROLYN. I know. I don't enjoy bored sex, either.

DAVID. Bored sex?

CAROLYN. Yes, bored. An-unexpected-hour-to-kill-we-might-as-well-have-sex sex. That's no fun for me.

DAVID. So . . . what I'm hearing is a no, then. Right?

CAROLYN. Tonight, much later, let's have some excellent-meal-and-great-wine-now-it's-time-for-sex sex. Ok? (*A beat.*)

DAVID. You'd rather go down to the bar for an hour.

CAROLYN. What's that supposed to mean?

DAVID. Nothing. That was just your suggestion, that's all.

CAROLYN. What was wrong with it?

DAVID. Nothing.

CAROLYN. You think I drink too much?

DAVID. No. (*A beat.*) I've never seen you drink too much.

CAROLYN. All right then. (*She goes and picks up the book emphat-*

*ically, sits on the bed and reads. He places his hand on her leg.*) What are you doing?

DAVID. Putting my hand on your leg.

CAROLYN. I'm trying to read. (*He removes his hand. She reads.*)

DAVID. Let's make love.

CAROLYN. No.

DAVID. Please? We'll do it real fast. Won't even take our clothes off.

CAROLYN. Why now? We have all weekend.

DAVID. (*Stroking her.*) I want to now. It's being in this same room . . .

CAROLYN. It's not the same room.

DAVID. It's close enough! It's the same hotel. It's the way you looked, on our honeymoon, sitting there.

CAROLYN. (*Pointing to the corner of the bed.*) You said I was sitting over there.

DAVID. It's the way you looked sitting, all right? Just sitting — it doesn't matter where. My God. It's the way you always look. You're attractive, for God's sake. (*A beat. She moves to him. Gives him a very good kiss.*)

CAROLYN. Thank you. Let's go to the bar.

DAVID. You look better now than you ever did. You know that? You're more beautiful than you've ever been.

CAROLYN. Thank you. (*She tries to rise; he gently pulls her back so that they are both reclining.*)

DAVID. I mean it. When I was young, I used to be terrified I'd marry someone whose body, as she got older, would . . . you know. And whose face would you know, too. I was afraid of what I'd do then. If that happened.

CAROLYN. David . . .

DAVID. 'Cause a lot of men do get out. They look at a woman they've been married to forever and . . . suddenly they just jump. They go and get a young girl. Look at Tom. He did. Debby's younger than his own daughter. I'm not saying she isn't nice in her own way, but . . . I liked Maureen. What do you think broke Tom and Maureen up, anyway?

CAROLYN. Maybe Maureen couldn't stand to watch Tom getting older. (*He laughs.*)

DAVID. There's an interpretation. (*A beat.*) Anyhow, I think you're beautiful.

135

CAROLYN. Thanks.

DAVID. Happy Anniversary.

CAROLYN. I'd like to get up. (*His hand still holds her.*)

DAVID. How did you get so beautiful, anyway?

CAROLYN. Maybe we should call Kevin.

DAVID. It's Friday night. There's probably not a kid in his whole dorm.

CAROLYN. Let's try him anyway.

DAVID. What's wrong?

CAROLYN. Nothing.

DAVID. I want to make love to you.

CAROLYN. I know that.

DAVID. Let me. (*She is silent. He begins kissing her face and neck, slowly. She remains impassive.*) You smell nice. Want me to talk about your smell for awhile?

CAROLYN. No. Thank you. (*A beat. He sighs, smiles.*)

DAVID. Ok, let's call Kev. (*He reaches for the phone.*)

CAROLYN. No . . . I guess I'd rather not.

DAVID. What do you want to do?

CAROLYN. Go to the bar. (*He moves away from the phone.*)

DAVID. Sure wish Tom and Maureen had stayed together.

CAROLYN. Don't we all.

DAVID. We had some great anniversaries. We'd go along with them, they'd come with us. It was almost like each couple was a little cheering section for the other. Congratulations. We've all made it another year. Now, with Debby, it's . . . (*He trails off. She picks up the book.*)

CAROLYN. Yes.

DAVID. Wasn't it terrible up in Stillwater last month? At the Lowell? God.

CAROLYN. Yes.

DAVID. She had him in their room all day. They only came out for meals. She just does it 'cause she's insecure. You and she don't have much to say to each other, do you?

CAROLYN. Not much.

DAVID. We won't have them along next year, all right? You think Tom'll mind?

CAROLYN. You tell me. He's your business partner. (*A beat.*)

DAVID. That book hasn't helped at all? "The Art Of Friendship"? In liking Debby, I mean?

CAROLYN. You think that's why I'm reading it?

DAVID. I don't know why you're reading it.

CAROLYN. Why are you reading it?

DAVID. 'Cause you're reading it. (*A beat. She reads. He moves to the window.*) Well, let's do our best to enjoy this weekend, eh? You're away from your work, I'm away from mine . . .

CAROLYN. (*Reading.*) Mm-hmm. (*He looks at her, then out the window.*)

DAVID. What's all that crap on Main Street? They having a fair tomorrow or something?

CAROLYN. I think so.

DAVID. (*Sitting, putting on his shoes.*) Red Wing, Minnesota. One of my favorite town names. Thoreau came here, you know.

CAROLYN. I know, it's in the brochure.

DAVID. The farthest north and west he ever traveled.

CAROLYN. I thought he got as far as St. Paul.

DAVID. He got as far as Minnesota, took one look, went home and died. Henry David Thoreau. Different drummer.

CAROLYN. What?

DAVID. Different drummer. Thoreau.

CAROLYN. Ah.

DAVID. Are you afraid of sex? (*She gives him an oh-come-on-now look. He looks out the window again.*) Well. 21 years. Our marriage is now an adult, eh? How've I been?

CAROLYN. What do you mean?

DAVID. As a husband. How've I been?

CAROLYN. Fine. You've been fine.

DAVID. Have you ever had an affair? (*A beat.*)

CAROLYN. No. Have you?

DAVID. No. (*A beat.*) I was just asking. (*A beat.*) I knew a guy once. Fellow I met at the club. He and his wife, for their 15th Anniversary, decided to admit all their extramarital affairs. They promised not to get mad—they had some kind of enlightened relationship. (*A beat.*) Anyhow, this happened one morning as she was taking him to work. They just drove along, trading infidelity stories, I guess. Trouble was, there got to be more infidelities than they thought. A lot more. (*A beat.*) As the numbers mounted, they began to get angry. It got to be real accusatory. He'd say, "You *what*?! With *who*?! How many's that, you immoral bitch!?" And she'd go, "Oh yeah? How many's that for

137

you, you piece of shit!?" (*A beat. He turns and looks at her.*) Right
about then she took her hand off the wheel and punched him in
the mouth. The car rolled over. They were both pinned inside.
They weren't hurt bad—well, he had a broken leg—but the doors
were all crushed in. Took a rescue team an hour to get 'em out.
(*A beat.*) The whole time they just kept yelling at each other
about all these affairs they'd had. They didn't even realize they'd
been in an accident. (*A beat.*) Are you having an affair?
CAROLYN. No.
DAVID. 'Cause if you were—I guess this is why I'm telling you
this story—if you were, I want you to know I'd never get violent
like that. It's not in me.
CAROLYN. Good. (*A beat.*)
DAVID. What's wrong? What's wrong here? I don't understand
what's wrong.
CAROLYN. Have I been acting different?
DAVID. I'm trying to be a good husband.
CAROLYN. I know.
DAVID. I'm trying to be sensitive to you. I want you to feel . . .
happy.
CAROLYN. Really?
DAVID. Yes. This is our weekend. We should be relaxing, we
should talk, we should be sensitive to each other.
CAROLYN. Why don't you be very sensitive to me right now,
and take me to the bar? (*A beat.*)
DAVID. I love you. I love you more now than I ever have. (*He
suddenly moves to his jacket, takes a small box out of the pocket, and puts
it on the bed.*) Here.
CAROLYN. What is it?
DAVID. It's for you. Take it. (*She does so, opens the box.*) It's an
engagement ring.
CAROLYN. We're married.
DAVID. It's for the next 20 years. Or 30, or whatever. It's to
thank you for all the good years we've had so far, and for all the
years we're going to have. In the future. As much as I love you
now, I'm going to love you more and more as we go on.
CAROLYN. David . . .
DAVID. You don't get uglier to me, you just get more beauti-
ful. If you like, we can get married again.
CAROLYN. I . . .

DAVID. You say I'm fine now, but I'm going to be perfect. You're going to have a perfect husband. We're going to fall deeper and deeper in love. (*A beat.*) Well? What do you say?

CAROLYN. I want a divorce. (*A motionless moment. Then, very softly, she closes the box.*)

DAVID. What?

CAROLYN. I want a divorce.

DAVID. I don't understand.

CAROLYN. I have to leave you.

DAVID. I don't know what you're talking about.

CAROLYN. I want a divorce. I have to . . .

DAVID. What the hell are you saying?! I'm giving you a ring here! (*She sets the ring down on the foot of the bed.*) You have a lover.

CAROLYN. No.

DAVID. You're not satisfied with me?

CAROLYN. That's not it.

DAVID. I'm talking about sex here . . .

CAROLYN. I know.

DAVID. Why do you want a divorce? Am I at work too much?

CAROLYN. No.

DAVID. 'Cause I can cut my time down at the agency. I can do that. Do I talk about my work too much?

CAROLYN. No. Well — no.

DAVID. I make a lot of money.

CAROLYN. I know.

DAVID. Kev likes me.

CAROLYN. Kevin loves you.

DAVID. Do you? (*A beat.*) I've bought you things. I have a sense of humor.

CAROLYN. Yes.

DAVID. What *is* it? Are you mad at me?

CAROLYN. I don't know. I wasn't prepared to talk about this . . .

DAVID. What were you going to do? Send a letter? (*A beat.*) Are you sick or something?

CAROLYN. No.

DAVID. Have you been seeing anyone? A therapist, or . . . ?

CAROLYN. No. I just have . . . problems with our being together.

DAVID. Problems. What are they? Let's work them out.

139

CAROLYN. I don't think we can work them out.

DAVID. Of course we can work them out.

CAROLYN. I don't want to work them out. (*A beat.*)

DAVID. I've always felt we had the kind of marriage that would allow us to talk over problems. Any problem. Isn't that true? (*A beat.*)

CAROLYN. I guess.

DAVID. I don't care how shameful or embarrassing or personal your problem is. You realize that.

CAROLYN. David . . . (*He silences her with a gesture, goes to the hall door, takes the "Do Not Disturb" sign from the inside handle, puts it on the outside handle, closes the door again, attaches the chain. He returns and sits.*)

DAVID. Is it alcohol?

CAROLYN. David.

DAVID. You keep wanting to go down to the bar . . .

CAROLYN. It's not that.

DAVID. Some kind of drug? Are you taking pills?

CAROLYN. No.

DAVID. I know lots of people who can help. A doctor at the Hazelden Center. I met him at the club.

CAROLYN. David . . .

DAVID. There's nothing bad about being addicted. He said so.

CAROLYN. I'm not . . .

DAVID. (*Takes her by the hands.*) 'Cause we all are. We smoke — we suck on burning plants, for God's sake. We drink — we pour poisonous liquids right down our throats . . . (*She pulls away.*) So. Is it alcohol?

CAROLYN. *I'm not addicted!* All right?

DAVID. (*Quietly.*) Of course you don't *think* you are. No addict ever thinks they're . . . (*She suddenly rises and goes into the bathroom.*) I can send you anywhere you want to go. The Betty Ford Institute? No problem. Say the word. It's a financial burden I'd be happy to bear.

CAROLYN. (*Off.*) I'm not going to the Betty Ford Institute.

DAVID. Why not? You'll meet famous people. Liz Taylor, Tony Curtis, Johnny Cash — they've all been there. You could get well *and* get autographs. (*She reenters, stands in the bathroom doorway.*)

CAROLYN. I'm going to the bar.

DAVID. (*Blocking her way.*) Honey—don't. You're just giving in to it . . .

CAROLYN. Damn it . . . !

DAVID. None of them asked for a drinking problem. No one ever does. That's why there's no shame in it. (*She sits, exhausted.*) That's why when I see Becky Lindquist fall asleep on the couch at one of our parties, I don't blame her. I help Dick pick her up and put her in the car. And I pray she'll go seek help.

CAROLYN. I do, too.

DAVID. Exactly.

CAROLYN. Do you really believe I have a drinking problem? (*A beat.*)

DAVID. No. (*He sits, not looking at her.*)

CAROLYN. I compare us to other couples. I know that's bad, but I do. In 21 years, I never saw a couple I'd rather be. I look at Tom and Debby. They look like a father and daughter who got confused. Like a teacher and student. Like she's studying for a course she can never pass. I don't know why I have to leave you, but I do.

DAVID. I'm trying to understand this. Everything you've said so far points to a pretty happy marriage. Two people who like each other, who look good to each other. Who suit.

CAROLYN. Yes.

DAVID. A son that's well brought up, in college. You'd agree that's pretty much the way it's been? That's not an unfair characterization?

CAROLYN. No.

DAVID. But you also say—even though it's been good—our marriage is now dead. (*A beat.*) You see the logical gap there?

CAROLYN. I can't stay in a relationship just because there's nothing wrong with it.

DAVID. *Why the hell not!?* That's exactly why people stay in marriages. They spend the first 25 years of their lives finding the person they have the least problems with. Then they marry them. (*A beat.*) I'm going to give Kev a call.

CAROLYN. What?

DAVID. Let's call Kev. We'll get him to drive down.

CAROLYN. Why?

DAVID. (*Going to the phone.*) He's our son. He should be here.

CAROLYN. What are you talking about?

DAVID. (*Getting out his address book.*) We'll go on a picnic tomorrow. Does that sound good?
CAROLYN. No.
DAVID. (*Dialing.*) Sure. Look, we'll go up there on Barn Bluff. You know, on all that grass that looks so soft from the road . . .
CAROLYN. Why do you want to do that?
DAVID. He's our son.
CAROLYN. I don't want him here.
DAVID. Of course you do.
CAROLYN. No, I don't.
DAVID. He'll make you feel better. He always makes you feel better.
CAROLYN. He doesn't always make me feel better . . .
DAVID. Of course he does; he's your son.
CAROLYN. I don't *like* him. All right? (*A beat.*)
DAVID. Of course you like him.
CAROLYN. I don't want him here.
DAVID. All right. (*He puts down the receiver. The phone rings. On the second ring he answers.*) Yes? Oh, Debby—what do you want? No, she can't. She's indisposed. What? No, she can't talk, she's lying down. She's not in pain, she's just . . . Look, I'm afraid we're not going to make it to dinner. Yeah, I'm sorry. You'll have to eat without us. No, I can't say why, it's just . . . Carolyn's—you know—lying down, and I'm . . . No, I can't say why. *Debby, she's indisposed, all right?! We're both indisposed!* (*He hangs up.*)
CAROLYN. (*Sarcastically.*) You suppose she thinks we're having a fight?
DAVID. Is this a joke? Is this something that Tom and Debby and you have all worked up to . . . ? (*He trails off.*)
CAROLYN. No.
DAVID. Then what *is* it?! What on earth is this?
CAROLYN. I can't . . . phrase it.
DAVID. Of course you can phrase it. Why can't you? Is it a secret?
CAROLYN. No.
DAVID. Are you having trouble with the language? Are you . . .
CAROLYN. *David* . . .
DAVID. For God's sake, you're a speech consultant. This is your work. It's what you do all day.
CAROLYN. This is not like my work.

142

DAVID. Yes, it is! It's talking! It's communication! All day you show businessmen how to present their cases, right? You show them how to gain trust, how to win a point. Well? Gain my trust. Win a point.

CAROLYN. Don't you think if I could, I would? (*A beat.*)

DAVID. Let's analyze this. Let's — let's work together, all right? There's no reason to approach this like we're on opposite sides. Let's just . . . just hone in on this as a team.

CAROLYN. I don't think . . .

DAVID. We're both professionals; this is easy. Look: for example, we'll start with the time factor. How long have you wanted a divorce? (*She sighs.*)

CAROLYN. I don't know. Not long. A week.

DAVID. A week? What happened a week ago?

CAROLYN. I read an article.

DAVID. An article? In what?

CAROLYN. I read a newspaper article.

DAVID. About relationships?

CAROLYN. No.

DAVID. What about?

CAROLYN. You'll think I'm being silly.

DAVID. I won't think you're being silly.

CAROLYN. Yes, you will.

DAVID. Will you tell me what the article was about!?

CAROLYN. Outer space.

DAVID. Outer space.

CAROLYN. That's right. It's silly.

DAVID. Oh, no. No. Outer space. That's not silly. Go on.

CAROLYN. It was about the new telescope they put up there. You know — the one that's . . . orbiting in outer space?

DAVID. All right.

CAROLYN. Well, the telescope is above the atmosphere, so it sees the universe more clearly, I guess. It's more sensitive. They're using it to re-see everything. And one of the first things they've discovered is a new body.

DAVID. A new body?

CAROLYN. A new heavenly body, that's . . . very big. And dark, instead of light. It's almost as big as the sun, but it doesn't shine. We never knew it was there. Until now. It's cold. Instead of heating up, it got cold. Or stayed cold, I guess.

DAVID. And this made you want a divorce?

CAROLYN. It's close, too. It's right next to our solar system. Right over our shoulder, they said, sort of. Dark, so we never knew it was there. (*A beat.*) When I read that, I felt like it was me being described. Like I . . . am that dark body.

DAVID. You are.

CAROLYN. Yes.

DAVID. That's it? That's the whole thing?

CAROLYN. Yes.

DAVID. Why are you leaving me?

CAROLYN. I just told you.

DAVID. You told Carl Sagan, that's who you just told. I'm not even sure you told him.

CAROLYN. I knew you'd say it was silly.

DAVID. It's not silly, it's ridiculous. You are not a "dark body." You're Carolyn Rich. You're married to David Franklin Rich. Remember? We're the Riches. We live in a nice suburb of a nice city in the nicest country on earth.

CAROLYN. *You* think it's nice.

DAVID. It's nice, goddammit! It's demonstrably nice! Read the crime statistics. Look at the neighbors, they look like you. They look like me. We fit in. We are not dark bodies! (*A beat.*) We'll find a nice counselor.

CAROLYN. I don't want to.

DAVID. No one leaves a marriage this way! "Good-bye, I read a space article, please hold the therapy"?

CAROLYN. David . . .

DAVID. These are modern times. We live in a high quality-of-life state. People work on their marriages up here.

CAROLYN. I just feel . . .

DAVID. You think we live in some Faulkner novel? You think we live in the South? This is the sanest part of the country. They have studies to prove it. Have you ever heard of the Minnesota Multi-Phasic Personality Profile? The *Minnesota* Multi-Phasic. Developed right here. People all over America take it, but *we* developed it. Because we are the measuring rod against which a nation is judged. I firmly believe that.

CAROLYN. I really don't see what . . .

DAVID. Hundreds of questions. Yes or no answers. Number two pencil. You can't lie to the test. You can't seem to be healthy.

There are too many infinitely fine shadings. You can lie to question 13, but question 237 will trip you up.

CAROLYN. David . . .

DAVID. Four hours long. "I feel like there's a tight steel band around my head." Yes or no. "My stools are black and tarry." Yes or no. "I am a superman." Yes or no. Did you ever take that test?

CAROLYN. Yes.

DAVID. Did you pass it?

CAROLYN. Yes. (*A beat.*)

DAVID. Why can't you give me a reason?!

CAROLYN. I don't know what it is. I can't say it in words. (*A beat.*)

DAVID. Say something. (*A beat.*)

CAROLYN. A couple of days ago I was driving past the lake. I was following a taxi, and we stopped at a light, and . . . in the back of the cab I could see two women about my age. One was ordinary. But the other one had on this red-and-white checked painter's hat — the most ridiculous hat possible for a woman that age. She was all excited, talking a mile a minute to her friend. She was retarded. You could tell by the way she moved her hands and touched her mouth while she talked. She seemed so aimless and happy. They were going to the beach together. They were going to swim. I've never seen a human being look so happy.

DAVID. And you wished you were . . . what? . . . as happy as her? (*She shakes her head no.*)

CAROLYN. As dignified. (*A long beat. She rises, goes to the armoire. She gets her travel bag out.*)

DAVID. What are you doing?

CAROLYN. Packing.

DAVID. Why are you doing that?

CAROLYN. I have to leave.

DAVID. We've just started talking about this. I have, anyway. (*As she starts to pack.*) What do you mean by "dignified"? Let's define our terms here.

CAROLYN. They're already defined.

DAVID. By who? By you? I know *I* haven't defined anything here tonight. I feel like I haven't got any power at all.

CAROLYN. How do you like it?

DAVID. Oh, no — now, that's bullshit. You have plenty of power.

145

You have a car, you have a budget, you work . . . (*As she moves to the bathroom.*) *What is wrong!?*
CAROLYN. *I don't know!* (*She exits into the bathroom.*)
DAVID. You do know. You do, and you won't tell me. You've given me a lot of sci-fi crap, but you haven't found a single thing wrong with me. Have you? Have you, Carolyn? (*She reenters with a smaller bag.*) Why is that? (*She continues packing.*) Am I perfect? (*She packs.*) Are you just afraid to say something? Are you afraid of what I'd do? (*She picks up her bags.*)
CAROLYN. Good-bye. (*She starts for the door. He grabs her bag away from her.*) David. (*A beat.*) David, give me some help on this.
DAVID. No.
CAROLYN. Please . . .
DAVID. You're not leaving here. Not till I say so. Not till I know why. I don't care if it takes a week. (*A beat. She grabs at her bag.*) *GET AWAY!!* (*He pulls it out of her reach.*)
CAROLYN. You can't force me to stay here. You can't. (*He stares at her, then puts the bag down in front of her.*)
DAVID. You're free to go. (*She picks up her bag tentatively. He makes no move.*) If you think you have the right to go without telling me why — in a way I can understand — then go. (*She hesitates.*) Go ahead. It's your life. (*A beat.*) If you stay, you're going to tell me. (*She closes her eyes, puts down her bag. She crosses to the corner of the bed and sits.*)
CAROLYN. You shit.
DAVID. Now we're getting somewhere. (*Lights fade to black. End of Scene One.*)


SCENE TWO

*Lights up on the same scene, an hour later.*

*It is now completely dark outside. David lies on the bed, talking on the phone, which he has brought over from the desk. His tie is loosened. Carolyn sits at the desk, writing — or rather, staring at a piece of paper, pencil in hand.*


DAVID. You're not sick or anything, are you? Good. You take care of yourself now. Eat right. Makes all the difference. What

146

are you doing home on a Friday night, anyway? Thought you'd be out with Janie, or . . . what? Ann? Oh, it's Ann now, isn't it? Sorry. Thought you'd be out with her. Oh, I see. (*To Carolyn.*) Ann went home for the weekend. (*To the phone.*) Why didn't you go with her? You've done that before, haven't you? Her folks like you. You two aren't having any trouble, are you? Good. (*To Carolyn.*) They're doing fine. (*To the phone.*) Why am I calling? Well, um . . . (*Laughs.*) Not sure, really. Your Mom and I were just sitting here, and . . . you know, talking about this and that, and . . . just thought we'd say hello. Got any problems? Need some money? No? Ok. (*A beat.*) What? Oh — sure, if you've got to get back to it, you gotta get back. You sound great. I'll tell your mother you love her. She says hello — she's waving from the bathroom. We're having a fabulous anniversary. Our anniversary, remember? Doesn't matter. You just, um . . . study. 'Bye. (*Hangs up.*) He's fine. (*A beat. He moves, tries to look over her shoulder at what she's writing; she pulls it away. He looks around, then idly examines a corner of the sheet.*) Same sheets. (*A beat.*) Same sheets, I said.

CAROLYN. What?

DAVID. The bed. It has the same brand of sheets as 20 years ago.

CAROLYN. It's not the same bed.

DAVID. I love this hotel. They really keep it up. When I was a kid, my Dad always used to show me the sheets whenever we went on a trip. Every motel and hotel. It was his business, linens.

CAROLYN. I know.

DAVID. "By their sheets shall ye know them." He would actually say that. This is a beautiful quality sheet. (*A beat.*) You know, I was in an Irish whorehouse once — just after college — and there they had mesh sheets. Mesh. Really. You could stick your fingers through them. Did I ever tell you about the Irish whorehouse?

CAROLYN. On our honeymoon.

DAVID. Dad wanted to be buried in a sheet. You know — wrapped up in a winding sheet, the old way. "Born in it, buried in it." That's what he used to say. Conceived in it, too, I suppose. (*A beat.*) Sure you don't want to forget all this and just come to bed? (*She gives him a look, then goes back to her writing. He rises.*) So — what've you got?

CAROLYN. Don't look yet.

DAVID. Why not? You've had nearly an hour.

CAROLYN. I'm not finished yet. (*A beat. He moves to another part of the room.*)

DAVID. You notice how much better shape Tom is in, since he married Debby? God, it's funny to watch him down at the club. He used to sit in the lounge watching ballgames. Now he's out there with me, screaming around the track for miles . . . We play racquetball, we swim, we powerlift. Hope Debby appreciates it. Then you know what he likes to do? When we're done? He likes to sit and watch the other guys walk by. I sit there with him. He looks for the out-of-shape guys—you know, for comparison. There's a lot of them, too. Men who've stayed with their wives, I guess. I don't know. It's quite a sight, though. Some of those guys are in real trouble. They look like pregnant women. You know, just a bunch of arms and legs designed to move a stomach around. It's disturbing, really. They're still clever, they're bright at work. But you watch their bodies become . . . chaotic. The flab just . . . cascades down over their necks, their elbows, their knees. They form breasts. These men . . . deform right before your eyes. People you once cared for. (*A beat.*) Not Tom, though. Not me, either. (*A beat.*) Look, are you hungry? We could call down for room service.

CAROLYN. No.

DAVID. We shouldn't skip dinner. (*Picks up a complimentary menu from a table.*) Look, there's a catfish thing they can send up.

CAROLYN. *No.* (*A beat.*)

DAVID. All right, time's up. What've you got? (*He picks up the paper she's been working on.*) There's only two sentences here.

CAROLYN. I know.

DAVID. That's all you wrote? In an hour?

CAROLYN. I think those are the main things.

DAVID. The main things?! (*Tosses the paper on the desk.*) We come up with more ideas in three minutes at work. Did you do it the way I told you?

CAROLYN. I tried . . .

DAVID. You're supposed to write down everything. No idea is bad. We sort them out later.

CAROLYN. Everything I thought of got back to these.

DAVID. You're going to leave me on the strength of two sentences, huh? Don't you see you're editing? You're editing your ideas before you present them. What am I supposed to do with just two sentences?

CAROLYN. You could read them. (*He picks up the paper, stares at her a moment, then hands her the paper.*)

DAVID. You read. Give me the full dramatic effect.

CAROLYN. The first sentence says, "You seem smaller to me."

DAVID. What?

CAROLYN. You seem smaller to me.

DAVID. Than what?

CAROLYN. Than you were. When we first married, you seemed . . . bigger. You were a bigger man.

DAVID. You mean I was more generous?

CAROLYN. No — *bigger*. Physically. Literally. You felt bigger.

DAVID. This is sex.

CAROLYN. No, it's not sex, it's . . . You seemed big and I seemed small. That's how it felt. Now I seem big and you seem small. (*A beat.*)

DAVID. Well, this is progress. You're leaving me because I seem small.

CAROLYN. Small*er*.

DAVID. Small*er*. Than I was. You seem bigg*er* . . .

CAROLYN. Yes.

DAVID. Than you were.

CAROLYN. That's right. (*Sincerely.*) Does that help?

DAVID. (*Angry, sarcastic.*) Are you kidding? Does it *help*?! *No*.

CAROLYN. I just mean when we . . . got married — when anybody gets married — they seem larger than . . . they really are, because of all the things they could be. All the things there are to find out about them. As the years go by. And then, *as* the years go by, all these things get found out. The people . . . explore the possibilities . . . of each other.

DAVID. And?

CAROLYN. And . . . the more they find out, the fewer . . . surprises they have left . . . to look forward to.

DAVID. You've explored me.

CAROLYN. Yes. Completely.

DAVID. Completely?

CAROLYN. Yes. (*A beat.*)

DAVID. It's not possible to know another human being completely.

CAROLYN. I wish that was true.

DAVID. You do not know me!

CAROLYN. I know what you'll do if I get sick. I know what you'll be like if you have a great day at work. I know how you eat a hamburger . . .

DAVID. How do I eat a hamburger?

CAROLYN. You go all the way around. You just keep going all the way around until there's nothing left. I know what you'd be like if I died. Or if Kevin died . . .

DAVID. That's morbid.

CAROLYN. I know what you'll do if I ask you to take me to a concert.

DAVID. What'll I do?

CAROLYN. You'll take me. I've spent 21 years discovering you, mapping you out, walking all the way to the borders of who you are. I've enjoyed it, but . . . now there's nothing left to explore.

DAVID. That's how you see it? That's marriage? You explore me, I explore you — and you get done first?

CAROLYN. David . . .

DAVID. How old are you?

CAROLYN. What?

DAVID. How old are you?

CAROLYN. You know how old I . . .

DAVID. I want to hear you say it.

CAROLYN. I'm 41.

DAVID. How old am I?

CAROLYN. David . . .

DAVID. How old?

CAROLYN. 45.

DAVID. We're halfway. More than halfway through our lives. Our son is full-grown. And whether we're tired of them or not, some things in our life have become worth holding onto.

CAROLYN. Why?

DAVID. Because they're ours! We made them! (*A beat.*) Even if this marriage is dead, it still has value.

CAROLYN. For who?

DAVID. For me. (*A beat. She suddenly pushes the desk over in a violent motion.*) What the hell?!

CAROLYN. *I do not belong to you!*

DAVID. I didn't say you did. (*She goes and sits in a corner of the room.*) Jesus. This is an expensive desk, you know. The whole room's expensive. Don't start tossing things around.
CAROLYN. Shut up.
DAVID. (*Righting the desk.*) Are you gay?
CAROLYN. What?
DAVID. Is that what it is? Have you discovered you're really . . . ?
CAROLYN. I take it back. You can still surprise me. With stupidity.
DAVID. I'll take what I can get. (*She sighs. We hear the sound of a train, slowly coming to a stop. He goes to the window, stares out.*) Amtrak. It's stopping. People waiting to get on. People getting off. Is this a tourist town?
CAROLYN. Thoreau came here.
DAVID. What would you do with your life? If we did break up?
CAROLYN. I don't know.
DAVID. Is that how you were going to get back home? Take the train?
CAROLYN. I was going to take the car. You were going to take the train.
DAVID. Oh. Great. Thanks. (*We hear the train pull out.*) There it goes again.
CAROLYN. (*Rising.*) I should leave.
DAVID. So I'm predictable? That's my problem?
CAROLYN. That's *the* problem. It's me, not you. Your possibilities for *me* are exhausted, not for someone else.
DAVID. I see. So now I should go get somebody else — now that I'm 45 — and hope that she won't get bored with me until we're both too decrepit to leave.
CAROLYN. I even knew how you'd react to this.
DAVID. Oh, you did, did you? Had me all mapped out?
CAROLYN. I knew you'd reject it, that you'd be sarcastic, that you'd . . .
DAVID. That I'd what?
CAROLYN. That you'd do anything except say you're sorry.
DAVID. Sorry? For what?
CAROLYN. For this. For what it's come to, for how unhappy I feel.
DAVID. I didn't make you unhappy! I did my best! Where do I get paid off for that? You don't hear "I'm sorry," eh? Well, I

151

don't hear, "Thanks." No—all I hear is that my wife is leaving me because I don't know six ways to eat a hamburger! (*The phone rings. He answers.*) Yes! What do you want, Tom? That's great—I'm glad you had a good dinner. Look, Carolyn's not feeling well . . . No, it's not her back. It's got nothing to do with her back. (*Putting his hand over the phone.*) He wants to give you an adjustment. (*To phone.*) Tom, you are not a doctor. Three years as a student manager for a hockey team doesn't make you a doctor. You can adjust my wife's spine until it turns to dust, but it won't cure her. Do you understand? *Tom, you are not a fucking doctor!* (*He slams the receiver down, then yanks the cord out of the wall and all in one motion throws the phone out the window. After a moment we hear it hit below.*)
CAROLYN. (*Rushing to the window.*) What are you doing?!
DAVID. Could you predict that?! Hah?! Could you?!
CAROLYN. You could've hit somebody!
DAVID. Did you know I was going to do that?!
CAROLYN. No! (*She looks out the window as he enters the bathroom.*) You broke their phone. It's all smashed to pieces!
DAVID. (*Off.*) I don't care!
CAROLYN. They're going to know who did it. The room number's on the phone. (*We suddenly hear glass shattering in the bathroom. She starts, moves toward the bathroom.*) David! (*He reenters before she gets to the door.*)
DAVID. It's all right. (*He goes and sits, a little mechanically, on the bed. She looks into the bathroom.*)
CAROLYN. You broke the mirror!
DAVID. Yes, I did.
CAROLYN. Why?
DAVID. Were you surprised? (*A beat.*)
CAROLYN. There's glass everywhere. What if someone heard?
DAVID. No one did. These old places are built like tombs.
CAROLYN. Well . . . they're going to find the phone.
DAVID. Let 'em! There are other hotels. This is a moveable feast. Besides, it fell in the alley. No one's going to find it right away. (*A beat.*) So. Is this a part of me you've already explored? Or not? Maybe we can just cross that sentence off the old list, eh? (*Picks up the list.*) What do you say? Didn't know I was capable of getting so angry at you, did you?

152

CAROLYN. You're not angry at me. I wish you were. There might be some hope, then.

DAVID. What the hell do you think I'm mad at?

CAROLYN. Losing.

DAVID. (*Knocking the desk over.*) That's *bullshit!*

CAROLYN. That's an expensive desk.

DAVID. (*Knocking over the desk chair.*) Fuck you! I am crossing the first sentence off your goddamn list and that is that! You understand? It is no longer a problem. There are huge regions in me you have never entered! There are caverns in me! There are deep, dark places, and I know where they are!

CAROLYN. You do.

DAVID. Yes, I do!

CAROLYN. Hit me.

DAVID. What?

CAROLYN. Go on, hit me. If I'm the one you're mad at, hit me — not the furniture. (*A beat.*)

DAVID. No.

CAROLYN. Why not? I want you to.

DAVID. I can't.

CAROLYN. *Why the hell not, you chickenshit!?* (*A beat.*)

DAVID. Someone taught me not to. When I was young.

CAROLYN. I know. (*A beat.*) Kiss me.

DAVID. I thought you wanted me to hit you.

CAROLYN. Hit me or kiss me. I'll take either one.

DAVID. I don't feel like kissing you.

CAROLYN. Don't you need to?

DAVID. No, I don't need to.

CAROLYN. I do. I need a great big kiss that says, "Honey, I will do whatever it takes to help you stay alive — including break up this marriage." So. Want to kiss me?

DAVID. No.

CAROLYN. I didn't think so. (*Taking the list.*) Nobody explores another person all alone. You only get in where they let you in. I never meant there wasn't more of you to find. I only meant I was tired of trying to find it alone. (*Drops the list into a wastebasket.*)

DAVID. So there's hope, then.

CAROLYN. Hope?

DAVID. There's more in me. You just said.

CAROLYN. David . . .

DAVID. (*Retrieving the list from the wastebasket.*) There is. There's more possibility. That's all I'm trying to prove here. What's the other thing on the list? I didn't do so bad with the first thing. What's the second thing?

CAROLYN. Honey, the point is . . .

DAVID. (*Angrily.*) The point is nothing. The point is what I say the point is. The point is I am not giving up and neither are you. If there's a way I can be that's better for you, I'll learn it. I'll be it.

CAROLYN. You can't . . .

DAVID. I will. You're my wife. You're worth fighting for. If not you, who else? Right? Now—what's the second thing?

CAROLYN. (*Reads.*) "I don't like your nose."

DAVID. You don't what?

CAROLYN. I don't like your nose. (*He stares at her, then snatches up the paper.*)

DAVID. You don't like my *nose?*

CAROLYN. (*Heading for the bathroom.*) No.

DAVID. What's wrong with it?

CAROLYN. (*Staring into the bathroom.*) It's full of glass.

DAVID. It's full of what?

CAROLYN. The bathroom! It's full of glass.

DAVID. I know, I broke the mirror.

CAROLYN. Well, I *can't pee!*

DAVID. What about my nose?!

CAROLYN. I don't care about your nose . . . !

DAVID. You sure as hell do! It's right here in black and . . .

CAROLYN. David! I can't pee!

DAVID. So?

CAROLYN. *Fix it!!* (*She suddenly starts crying and sits. He watches her a moment, then goes into the bathroom. We hear him kicking glass out of the way, tossing shards into the tub. She cries as hard as she can. He reenters, quietly.*)

DAVID. It's ok now. (*Takes a step toward her.*) You can go. I cleared a path for you.

CAROLYN. I'm sorry.

DAVID. What for? For yelling? You had every right.

CAROLYN. I'm sorry that I ever told you. That I didn't just . . . live with you the rest of my life.

DAVID. Why?

CAROLYN. Because you can't help it. (*She slowly rises, goes into the bathroom, closes the door. A moment passes, in which he examines his nose. He does this delicately, thoughtfully. He rises, approaches the door uncertainly, then speaks to her through it in a respectful tone.*)

DAVID. Honey? I guess I'm just a little puzzled, that's all. About what you mean when you say you don't like my nose. Is it . . . is it the shape? (*No answer.*) Is it . . . the size? (*No answer.*) Is it the hair? I'll use a tweezers if you want. (*No answer.*) What is it? (*She reenters.*)

CAROLYN. The way you blow it. (*She goes to the hall door.*)

DAVID. The way I blow it? (*She opens the door, looks out.*) Where are you going?

CAROLYN. Nowhere. They really didn't hear you break the mirror, did they? I wonder what's going on in their rooms. (*Closes the door.*) When you blow your nose, you take a handkerchief, very neatly unfold it, and give a big blow. Then you give three little blows right in a row. Then you fold your handkerchief back up neatly and put it away.

DAVID. So?

CAROLYN. I used to love that. That whole little ritual. It was simple, and efficient—even elegant in its own silly way.

DAVID. Well, what's wrong? I still do it.

CAROLYN. I know. And somehow, over the years, that little ritual—which you've never changed—bothers me.

DAVID. It bothers you. A lot?

CAROLYN. It makes me want to pull my face off.

DAVID. Oh.

CAROLYN. It's not that the ritual itself is good or bad. It's just that, having seen it for 21 years . . .

DAVID. I'll stop doing it. I will.

CAROLYN. It's a habit.

DAVID. I'll break it.

CAROLYN. You can't break a . . .

DAVID. I'll break the goddamn habit! Jesus.

CAROLYN. It's not your only habit. You have others.

DAVID. What are they? I'll break those, too.

CAROLYN. No one can break all their habits.

DAVID. All my . . . ? *All?*

CAROLYN. Nearly all. For God's sake—there must be habits

155

of mine you can't stand. Things you used to like, but now . . .
DAVID. Yeah, but . . .
CAROLYN. So . . . maybe I don't want to change them. Maybe I can't. The point is, people begin to dislike the very things they used to like about each other. The things that attracted them in the first place. Things we're the most proud of — that we'd never want to give up. There are hundreds of things about you — things which you think make you great — that I hate more than anything in the world now.
DAVID. Let's change them.
CAROLYN. We can't change them.
DAVID. Why not?
CAROLYN. They're us, that's why. They're everything about us. They're who we've become.
DAVID. Can you name any others?
CAROLYN. You always say "Yes" when you answer the phone. You drive with one hand. You call our son Kev. You've used the same deodorant for 21 years. On Fridays you like to make love from behind.
DAVID. That it?
CAROLYN. Your left ear is lower than your right. You never look my mother in the eye. You surprise me with a romantic gesture once every four months.
DAVID. There's a lot of these, aren't there?
CAROLYN. Yes.
DAVID. These are things you can't stand anymore?
CAROLYN. I'm sorry.
DAVID. Some people stay married 50 years. How do they manage it?
CAROLYN. I think . . . by pretending to be dead. They don't listen to each other. They don't look at each other, they don't think . . . about each other. They're just together. Like us.
DAVID. We're not like that.
CAROLYN. We are.
DAVID. We'll change.
CAROLYN. David . . .
DAVID. I mean it. I'll change. I'll . . . Whatever person you need me to become, I'll become. Just tell me what you want.
CAROLYN. That's ridiculous.

DAVID. It's not ridiculous! Leaving without trying is ridiculous. Leaving because you're afraid to become something new is ridiculous.

CAROLYN. You can't just . . .

DAVID. A new man. A whole new man. At no cost. If you don't like my behavior, I'll adjust it. If you don't like my clothes, I'll get new clothes. If you want me to have a little facial surgery . . .

CAROLYN. David . . .

DAVID. I'll do it. Our son is Kevin from now on. I'll say hello on the telephone.

CAROLYN. Stop this.

DAVID. What about politics? I could vote socialist or something . . . (*She picks up her bag.*) Where are you going?

CAROLYN. Out.

DAVID. You've got to make a new man of me.

CAROLYN. I can't.

DAVID. *I* can. You help. We'll both work on it. We'll each of us become new. New man, new woman. Kevin'll never recognize us.

CAROLYN. You've solved another one, haven't you? Just like putting together a big ad campaign. Analyze the problem, arrange all the elements, reach a solution. A little trouble with the marriage? Just find out what's on her mind, learn the vocabulary of her complaint, find out what will calm her down . . .

DAVID. I'm looking for a creative response to this.

CAROLYN. . . . look for a creative response . . .

DAVID. *Carolyn.*

CAROLYN. (*Throwing her bag at him.*) *I am not a little problem!*

DAVID. Hey!

CAROLYN. You're not going to put in a day or two of acting different, just so we can go back to the same old routine!

DAVID. I didn't mean . . .

CAROLYN. You didn't mean what?! You didn't mean to kill our marriage? I didn't either, but that's what we did!

DAVID. I never killed this marriage. I loved you. I love you right now.

CAROLYN. *So what!?* I've loved you, too — every minute. What good is that?

DAVID. What *good* is it? That's all there is: loving. Being together, talking, asking questions. If there's a problem, I ask questions. If they're not the right questions, I ask more. Are these the right questions?

CAROLYN. Yes.

DAVID. Then why can't you answer them?

CAROLYN. They're in the wrong language. (*A beat.*) Language goes between two people. We . . . lost ours. We're just a lovely couple now. Having an argument, discussing an issue, going to dinner, driving in a car — it doesn't matter. We're a blank. We don't exist. You can't ask a question I can understand. I can't give you an answer. (*A beat. She goes and picks up her bag.*) I wish I could. I wish there was a language. But there isn't. I need the car keys.

DAVID. What?

CAROLYN. I need the car keys.

DAVID. I'm sorry, I don't understand you.

CAROLYN. David.

DAVID. Must be some problem with the language. Maybe if you gestured . . .

CAROLYN. Damn it, give me the keys! (*A beat. He stares at her intensely.*)

DAVID. Which car do you want?

CAROLYN. What?

DAVID. Which car? The Pontiac or the Volvo?

CAROLYN. We only have one car down here.

DAVID. But eventually. Ultimately. Which car?

CAROLYN. Give me the keys . . .

DAVID. Which car?

CAROLYN. I don't care. The Volvo.

DAVID. I want the Volvo.

CAROLYN. Then the Pontiac.

DAVID. I want the Pontiac. I want the Pontiac and the Volvo. (*A beat.*)

CAROLYN. All right. (*She reaches out for the keys.*)

DAVID. What about the finches?

CAROLYN. The finches?

DAVID. The finches. Kevin's allergic to dogs, so we have three finches. I want two of them.

CAROLYN. Fine. Take any two you want. I'll leave both cars in the garage. All right? Just give me the keys.

DAVID. Actually, I want all three finches.

CAROLYN. *Take them! Take the fucking finches!* (*He slaps her. She falls on the bed.*)

DAVID. Don't raise your voice to me! We are not just a "lovely couple"! We have emotions! We're bristling with 'em! I'm intensely aware that I exist! I have spaces in me! I have areas!

CAROLYN. I thought you couldn't hit people.

DAVID. I can't! (*A beat. Slowly she sits, then stands.*)

CAROLYN. I have to go now, honey . . . (*He slaps her again.*) Why are you *hitting* me?!

DAVID. I don't know! You keep trying to leave.

CAROLYN. I have to leave! (*They stare at each other.*) You let me go now.

DAVID. No.

CAROLYN. I'm your wife. You let me go. (*A beat.*)

DAVID. No.

CAROLYN. I'll fight to get out.

DAVID. I don't care.

CAROLYN. I'll win.

DAVID. I don't care. (*She bows her head, starts crying.*) Don't. Don't do that. Carolyn, don't . . . (*She suddenly lunges at him with a yell, and manages to knock him back, so that he trips and falls. Quickly, she kicks him in the side.*)

CAROLYN. *Goddamn you!*

DAVID. Aggghhh! (*He rolls away and begins to stand. She kicks him in the shin and he falls again.*)

CAROLYN. How dare you still want me! How dare you!

DAVID. I do . . .

CAROLYN. You have spaces!? You want 'em filled?! I'll fill 'em for you! (*She kicks him in the side again.*)

DAVID. Aggh!

CAROLYN. Are you going to let me out of this room!?

DAVID. Yes! Go! Please! (*He holds out the keys to her. She takes them.*)

CAROLYN. All right. I'm sorry I had to get upset with you.

DAVID. (*Still on the floor, holding his side.*) Get *upset*?

CAROLYN. (*Picking up her bag.*) I suppose it's progress that you could bring yourself to slap me. I'm not sure if it makes me want to thank you or kill you.

DAVID. Thank me.

CAROLYN. The train comes again tomorrow morning. Or maybe Tom and Debby'll give you a ride. I should be gone by the time you're home. (*A beat.*) Well. Here's to a calm divorce. (*She moves past him on her way to the door. He grabs her leg, twists it and topples her, bags and all.*) NO!! (*He scrambles on top of her and hits her hard in the face with his open hand. There should be nothing stylized about this or any of the violence. It is serious and brutal. He hits her again. She lies unconscious. He rises slowly, takes the keys from her hand.*)

DAVID. We're going to have a lousy divorce. We're going to fight over the house, the furniture, the cars. I'm never going to pay alimony. Kevin is . . . *Kev* is going to blame you, not me. I'm going to date other girls. (*He moves to the window, looks out.*) Fucking phone's still down there. I gotta pee. (*He stumbles into the bathroom. We hear glass being kicked along the tile floor. Carolyn opens her eyes. She feels her face, winces with pain. There is a small amount of blood. We hear him urinating as she struggles to a standing position. She tries somewhat blindly to retrieve her bag and the keys. She goes to the night table and takes the book. She moves toward the hall door with her things as we hear him finish.*) God. That's better. That is a whole lot better. (*On this line, she has turned from the hall door and held the book up. He enters, still zipping up, on the last "better" — and she immediately strikes him hard in the head with the book.*) God . . . ! (*They disappear into the bathroom. We hear sounds of a struggle: glass flying around, two or three more blows, etc. Then silence. The whole thing takes only a few seconds. After a moment, she reappears — book still in hand. She staggers.*)

CAROLYN. There. You sleep in there tonight. (*Weakly, she tosses the book back into the bathroom.*) Here's a book. (*She reaches down for her bag, one eye closed now from the fighting, but she can't find the keys.*) All right, David. What'd you do with the keys? Come on . . . no more tricks . . . (*A wave of dizziness comes over her. She sits on the bed.*) I'm going to sit here a minute. (*She lies down across the bed.*) I'm going to lie down. (*A beat.*) Then later . . . I'm going to get up. (*Lights fade to black. End of Scene Two.*)

SCENE THREE

*Lights rise on the same scene, predawn the next morning. Carolyn still lies on the bed, but now she lies the normal way, with her head on the pillow. The lamp on the night table is on. Her eyes — one of which is black — are closed. She is motionless. Her bag, her coat on top of it, has been set neatly by the hall door. The rest of the room is as it was.*

*After a moment, the hall door opens and David appears. He, like Carolyn, is dressed as he was last night. He is disheveled, with a bandage just above his temple. His face is bruised, and he favors his hand. He carries in his good hand the telephone he threw out the window. It is badly cracked, coming apart in places. He moves with some difficulty. He stares at her, shuts the door behind him with his foot. He moves toward the bed, setting the phone down on the vanity as he passes, and plugging it in. He stands by the bed, staring at her. He turns off the light on the night table. He goes to the armoire, takes his bag out, tosses his clothes into it. He goes into the bathroom, comes out with his shaving kit.*

*The phone rings, with a muffled, broken sound. He is surprised, but does not move toward it. It rings five times as he puts his kit into his bag. He moves toward the straight chair and takes his jacket from off the back. As he does so, Carolyn slowly rises on one elbow watching him. He has not seen her. He tries to put on his jacket, but groans with the pain of trying to raise his arm, and desists. He puts his coat over his arm, takes his bag and starts for the hall door. He suddenly stops, awkwardly pulls the car keys from his pocket and sets them down on her bag and coat.*

*He turns, and for the first time sees her awake. He puts down his coat and bag, goes and sits on the edge of the bed, facing away from her. They do not look at each other. She touches his forearm. He rises, goes and picks up his coat. He stops, staring at the door. Drops his coat.*

*She delicately feels her bad eye, wincing at her own touch. He looks around, watches her. After a moment, she looks up and holds his gaze. Her hand drops into her lap.*

*He sits on the bed again. He puts his hand up to touch her near her eye. She flinches, then remains perfectly still as he inspects her bruise. Slowly, his hand moves down over her shoulder to her arm. The two of them lean awkwardly together, in a formal embrace.*

*She suddenly shifts out of the embrace, and stands unsteadily. She sees the box with the engagement ring at the end of the bed. She stares at it a moment, then picks it up, takes it to the desk and sets it there. She pauses, then returns to the bed. She sits, then lies back slowly, on her side, facing him. He looks at the box, then slowly lies back himself, staring ahead. Slowly their hands clasp. They look at their hands.*

*Lights fade to black.*

## THE END

# ELEEMOSYNARY

*A Play in Seven Scenes*

*To my wife Jeanne*

*Eleemosynary* was given its professional premiere at the Philadelphia Festival Theatre For New Plays, from April 29 to May 10, 1986. It was directed by Gloria Muzio; scenery was designed by Eric Schaeffer; costumes were designed by Vickie Esposito; lighting was designed by Curt Senie; sound design was by Jeff Chestek. The cast was as follows:

ECHO . . . . . . . . . . . . . . . . . . . . . . . . . . . . . . . . . Julie Boyd
DOROTHEA . . . . . . . . . . . . . . . . . . . . . . . . Lenka Peterson
ARTIE . . . . . . . . . . . . . . . . . . . . . . . . . . . . . . . Cynthia Mace

*Eleemosynary* was originally commissioned by Park Square Theatre of St. Paul, Minnesota and produced by them in August, 1985. It was directed by Jeanne Blake. Rick Polenek designed the set. The cast was as follows:

ECHO . . . . . . . . . . . . . . . . . . . . . . . . . . . . . . Michele Conlin
DOROTHEA . . . . . . . . . . . . . . . . . . . . . Mez Van Oppen
ARTIE . . . . . . . . . . . . . . . . . . . . . . . . . . . . . Lynn Musgrave

The author would like to gratefully acknowledge the National Endowment for the Arts, the Jerome Foundation, and the McKnight Foundation, without whose generous support this play could not have been written.

## AUTHOR'S NOTES

Dorothea should be played by an actress in her 50's
Artie should be played by an actress in her 30's
Echo should be played by an actrress in her teens

The preferred convention for performance of this play would have all books—and a pair of homemade wings—actually present. All other props (including phones) would be mimed or simply suggested by the context. Perhaps Dorothea could have a real pair of scissors in Scene 5.

## THE SET

This play works best when the setting is minimal. It should exist primarily in ever-shifting areas of light and darkness, with as few platforms, chairs, stools or whatever as possible. Artie's wings, which are much used and referred to, might profitably be incorporated into the set design, so as to remain a visual presence throughout.

# CHARACTERS

DOROTHEA. . . . . . . . . . . . . . . . . a woman of some means

ARTIE. . . . . . . . . . . . . . . . . . . . . . . . . . . . . . her daughter

ECHO. . . . . . . . . . . . . . . . . . . . . . . . . her granddaughter

## TIME

1985, and before

# Scene 1

*A girl of sixteen appears. It is Echo. She wears jeans and a white sweater.*

ECHO. Eleemosynary. E-L .. E-E ... M-O-S ... Y ... N-A-R ... Y. Eleemosynary. It's my favorite word. Not just because I won with it, either. It was always my favorite. Eleemosynary. "Of or pertaining to alms; charitable." It's from the Latin, of course, but it's our word now. We're responsible for it. Eleemosynary. Like a small song. *(D., lights slowly come up on Dorothea, lying motionless on a low platform. Echo slowly approaches her, studies her for a moment, then speaks to the audience.)* This is my grandmother. She had a stroke.

DOROTHEA. *(Unmoving, her eyes still closed.)* Could you open the drapes, dear?

ECHO. *(Miming opening the drapes.)* She can't really talk. I can hear her, though. At least I think I can. *(Sunlight catches Dorothea's face. She smiles, eyes still closed.)*

DOROTHEA. Oh, that's nice. That's warm.

ECHO. She's seventy-five years old. I know she doesn't look it. That's not how I see her.

DOROTHEA. I feel fifty today.

ECHO. I know. *(U. Artie enters. On her arms she wears a pair of large wings, made of lightweight wood and fabric. Each is perhaps two or three feet long. As Echo continues to speak, Artie stands still U. with the wings at her side, looking very unhappy. Dorothea rises and walks U. next to Artie.)* My grandmother believed she could fly using only a pair of homemade wings and the proper classical training. In 1958 she made a ten-minute movie—fully professional—of herself and her daughter, my mother, trying it out.

167

DOROTHEA. *(Speaking with force and assurance, as though to a film camera.)* Hello. I am Dorothea Wesbrook. Today I am going to prove that man — or, in this case, woman — can fly without the aid of any motor of any kind, using only the simple pair of wings you see my daughter, Artemis, wearing here. *(Artie, looking very self-conscious, begins to edge off camera. Dorothea stops her gently without interrupting her speech.)* We have an excellent day for the attempt. A bright, golden sky, a brisk wind and air temperatures in the high forties. We will try two experiments today. First, the very steep hill, and second, the wooden tower.

ECHO. Sometimes I think all my troubles began in 1958.

DOROTHEA. I wish I could be flying myself, but arthritis has made that impossible. Is the camera going? Splendid. Artie...

ARTIE. Mom...

DOROTHEA. Remember all I've taught you. *(A beat. Then suddenly Artie raises the wings up dramatically. She and Dorothea freeze in tableau.)*

ECHO. Spelling the words becomes easy, really — almost a nuisance N-U-I-S-A-N-C-E nuisance. What I really concentrate on is the meaning of the word — or more than that, the *feel* of it.

DOROTHEA. *(Annunciatory, to the "camera" as Artie flaps at first slowly, then faster and faster.)* The world is filled with an inner conviction. A cord of truth and power which needs only to be unsnarled and drawn taut between its center and our own! *(Dorothea's tone grows more and more dramatic. Artie gives a low, crescendoing wail and runs flapping across the stage at top speed. She exits. Dorothea freezes as before.)*

ECHO. Lots of words have a special feel. Words like prink and zenana. Words like dysphemism and autochthonous. Spelling them is nothing compared to just feeling them.

DOROTHEA. *(Suddenly shouting.)* Flap! For God's sake, you call that flapping?! You're being filmed! *(She freezes again.)*

ECHO. Beautiful words for ugly things. Limicolous. L-I-M-I-C-O-L-O-U-S. Limicolous. Means, "dwelling in mud." Or this one: Esurient. Just mean hungry. But the way it *feels.* I used to stop right in the middle of spelling it. Esurient. E-S-U-R-I ... There are words I'd give my life for.

DOROTHEA. *(As before.)* You're not concentrating!

ECHO. I still have the film my grandmother made.

ARTIE. *(Reentering, running, flapping.)* It's not working!

DOROTHEA. Keep trying! Concentrate!

ARTIE. I'm not flying!

DOROTHEA. You will! *(Artie gives another wail and exits flapping, as before.)*

ECHO. Mom was only fifteen then. This wasn't the first strange thing Grandma made her do.

ARTIE. *(Flapping and running back onstage, suddenly dropping the wings to her side, and speaking for the first time like a woman in her thirties, to the audience.)* Never have a daughter. Never have a child, for that matter, but *never* have a daughter. She won't like you.

DOROTHEA. Keep flapping! *(Artie wails again, and runs off flapping.)*

ECHO. My mom's a very intense person. I think it was her upbringing.

DOROTHEA. Artie! Remember! Inner conviction! *(Artie enters, sans wings. She speaks on the phone.)*

ARTIE. How are you coming on N, O and P? Is this a good time to call you?

ECHO. *(Doing the same.)* Fine. Mom, we don't have to do this if you don't want. Grandma can always help.

ARTIE. No, no, no — I've got the time. Honest. *(Picks up a dictionary.)* I've got my dictionary right here.

ECHO. Ok.

ARTIE. Good. Um ... periptery.

ECHO. We could just talk, if you'd rather.

ARTIE. Come on, periptery. "Region of air surrounding a moving body."

ECHO. Periptery. P-E-R-I-P-T-E-R-Y. Periptery.

ARTIE. Good. Um ... nyctitropic.

ECHO. What?

ARTIE. Nyctitropic.

ECHO. That's a word?

ARTIE. Of course it's a word. I see it in my work all the time.

ECHO. What's it mean?

ARTIE. "Tending to assume at nightfall positions unlilke those during the day." Like the leaves of certain plants.

ECHO. That's a scientific word. They don't ask those much.

ARTIE. Oh, they don't? I'm sorry. Well, then ... um...

ECHO. I'll do it anyway.

ARTIE. Can you? Do you know it?

ECHO. I can guess. Um ... nyctitropic. N-Y-C-T-I-T-R-O-P-I-C. Nyctitropic.

ARTIE. That's right! That's amazing! How do you do that?! *(Quickly paging through the book again.)* Now, let's see ... um ... um...

ECHO. Mom? Mom?

ARTIE. What?

ECHO. Let's just talk.

ARTIE. We are talking.

ECHO. Why don't you come over *here* and help me?

ARTIE. Well, um ... I'm very busy these days. You've got Dorothea, and...

ECHO. I want you too.

ARTIE. You've got me. You do. I'm right here. On the phone. Let's do another word. How about ... oh, I don't know ... um ... anything really. How about orbit?

ECHO. Orbit? You mean, like planets?

ARTIE. That's right.

ECHO. You think I can't spell orbit?

ARTIE. Just spell it and we'll go on, all right?

ECHO. Could you just please come over?

ARTIE. No. Orbit.

ECHO. Mom...

ARTIE. Orbit or I'm hanging up.

ECHO. *(After a beat.)* O-R-B-I-T. Orbit.

ARTIE. *(Quietly.)* Thank you. *(Lights fade on Artie. She exits.)*

ECHO. There's something about the Wesbrook women. We have this expectation about ourselves. To be extraordinary. It's a little like having a disease in the family. *(Artie returns during the above speech, with the wings again. She stands beside Dorothea. Artie looks exhausted once more, and once more is fifteen.)*

DOROTHEA. *(To camera.)* Well, the very steep hill seems not to have done the trick. We are moving on, therefore, to the wooden tower. *(Artie gives Dorothea an "Are you serious?" look. They freeze.)*

ECHO. When I was still in my crib, my grandmother was constantly shoving words and numbers in front of me. The first thing I ever said was the ancient Greek word for grandma.

DOROTHEA. *(To audience.)* My granddaughter is a born genius.

ECHO. Dorothea raised me from the time I was two. I could do calculus when I was nine.

ARTIE. I am *not* jumping off that tower.

DOROTHEA. Of course you are, dear.

ARTIE. You said this would be safe.

DOROTHEA. It is safe. Look at the tower's base. We've piled up dry leaves.

ARTIE. *Dry leaves?!*

DOROTHEA. *(To the camera, with impressive control.)* There will be a slight delay. *(They freeze.)*

ECHO. My grandmother made me love words. My mom helped, too. A little.

DOROTHEA. *(To Artie.)* Are you my daughter or not?

ECHO. At twelve, I decided to be the greatest speller in history. For life. I didn't realize only kids had spelling bees. I thought there was an adult division. *(Artie moves into position on the "tower.")*

DOROTHEA. *(To the camera, as Artie returns to fifteen.)* My daughter is now, oh, about twelve feet above the ground, and ... Let go of the railing, dear.

ARTIE. *(Eyes closed.)* No!

DOROTHEA. Don't be stubborn.

ECHO. Dorothea was one of the notable eccentrics of her time.

171

DOROTHEA. You want to fly, don't you?

ARTIE. No!

ECHO. I do.

DOROTHEA. Well, then you must let go.

ECHO. I fly with words. Oh, I know it sounds stupid to say, but it's true. Certain words literally lift me up to a ... private altitude. Sortilege, charivari, ungulate, favonian. And the word that means "playing with words" — logodaedaly. Isn't that a great one? Logodaedaly. It's a one-word yodel.

DOROTHEA. Why are you so afraid to make history?

ARTIE. *(Still holding onto the "railing.")* No daughter of mine will ever ... no daughter of *mine*...

DOROTHEA. Artie?

ECHO. *(Suddenly distraught, thirteen on the phone.)* Mom? Mom? Are you there?

ARTIE. What, honey?

ECHO. Could you come over?

ARTIE. Oh, I ... can't right now. What's wrong?

ECHO. *(Glumly.)* I'm the National Spelling Bee Champion.

ARTIE. *(Putting aside the wings.)* I know. You can be very proud of a year's work.

ECHO. What'll I do next year?

ARTIE. What do you mean?

ECHO. There's nothing left to spell. I spelled everything. I spelled zeugma and withershins and graupel and fogdog. I spelled revenant and arataxy. I even spelled phthisis. P-H-T-H-I-S-I-S. Phthisis. *(The last word is pronounced "tis-is." A beat.)* Could you *please* come over?

ARTIE. Echo, no.

ECHO. I even spelled eleemosynary. Just like it was cat or dog. I took a beautiful, amazing mechanism and *spelled* it.

DOROTHEA. *(Still looking up at the "tower.")* Artie?

ARTIE. *(Quietly.)* Don't take a negative attitude.

DOROTHEA. *(As before.)* Don't take a negative attitude.

ECHO. Why not? I turned those words into something nugatory and ugsome.

ARTIE. Into what?

ECHO. I made them derendipitous and marmoreal.

ARTIE. Damn it, speak English.

ECHO. I *am*. Those are good English words.

ARTIE. Some words are meant to be spelled, not used.

ECHO. I think spelling bees are the quiddity of hebetude! *(She exits. Artie dons the wings, stands beside Dorothea.)*

DOROTHEA. *(Into the camera, embarrassed.)* Well, um ... it appears we will not be able to complete our experiment today.

ARTIE. *(Eyes closed, holding on.)* Damn right.

DOROTHEA. What a pity. Hopefully, perhaps tomorrow...

ARTIE. Forget it.

DOROTHEA. You came so close on the hill...

ARTIE. Never! You are nuts! And now you're nuts on film! *(They freeze. Echo enters from another direction.)*

ECHO. Mom apologized for that later. Grandma never mentioned it again. She went right on to other projects: communication with the dead, spontaneous combustion, astral projection — but she never filmed those.

ARTIE. I'm sorry.

DOROTHEA. *(Moving toward the D. platform.)* That's all right. I forgive you. *(Artie exits as Dorothea lies down.)*

ECHO. I can feel my grandmother in me. My mother, too — a little. Something flies straight through us, straight from Dorothea to me. It's a gift.

DOROTHEA. The secret of flight lies in the assurance that we are worthy of flying.

ECHO. I guess it's a gift. *(Lights fade slowly to black.)*

## Scene 2

*Artie is alone onstage. She sits, smoking a cigarette.*

ARTIE. You don't have to smoke, but it makes you more forceful. Whoever's with you knows that while you do need oral gratification, you don't necessarily need it from them. *(A beat.)* I have trouble touching my daughter. I have trouble touching most people, but I don't worry about that. It's my daughter that worries me. *(Lights rise on the D. platform. Echo lies on it looking straight up. She has the blankly expectant look of an infant in her crib — which she is. Dorothea sits nearby her, smiling beautifully.)*

DOROTHEA. Are we all waked up from our nap? Are we, little Miss? *(She pokes Echo as she speaks, and Echo responds with laughter.)* We're all waked up and we're three months old, and we're ready to go to *school.*

ARTIE. Dorothea could touch her all day long.

DOROTHEA. *(Tickling Echo.)* Do we like school? Do we? Of course we do. Listen, Artie — how much she likes the thought of school. she's laughing.

ARTIE. She's laughing because you're tickling her.

DOROTHEA. Well, I'm sure that's part of it. *(To Echo, playing with an invisible baby's toy alphabet, hung over the "crib.")* Do we know this letter? That's "A". Can you say "A?" *(Echo gurgles happily.)* All right, how about this one? "B." That's right, that's "B." Can you say that?

ARTIE. Mom, She's three months old. She can't talk yet.

DOROTHEA. How do you know?

ARTIE. It's physiologically impossible.

DOROTHEA. That's just the truth of the body. Not the truth of the spirit. Echo, how about this one? "C."

ARTIE. Her name's not Echo.

DOROTHEA. Of course it is. I named her.

ARTIE. *I* named her. Months ago. I named her Barbara.

DOROTHEA. *(Smiling pleasantly.)* That was before I got here. Echo? Do you want to try these? *(Dandling another string of "letters.")* This is "Alpha." Can you say that? And this is "Beta." Can you say...? *(Dorothea and Echo freeze.)*

ARTIE. Those baby alphabets she's playing with are the same ones she had over my crib. Pink for Latin, blue for Greek.

DOROTHEA. *(Unfreezing, though Echo doesn't.)* "Lambda." Can you say "lambda?" Think of a little lamb.

ARTIE. *Mom, she can't talk!*

DOROTHEA. You certainly sound cross this morning. You should take a good long walk. That's what I do, when I'm feeling needlessly aggressive. Go on. Maybe you'll meet someone important or famous. I always do.

ARTIE. Who do you meet that's famous?

DOROTHEA. Last week I met President James Monroe.

ARTIE. You did?

DOROTHEA. Yes. It was really very fortunate, too. I had been meaning to ask President Monroe about the Era of Good Feelings. That's what they called his Presidency, you know — the Era of Good Feelings. It was from 1817 to 1825, and I picture it as one of the happiest times: The Era of Good Feelings. So I asked him — "Was it as good as all that?"

ARTIE. What did he say?

DOROTHEA. He said it was fair. I think he was just being modest. He was a good-looking man. The last president to wear short pants. Did you know that? He looked a little funny in this neighborhood, but all in all it was a very nice visit. So — have a walk, why don't you? Good for the post-partum nonsense.

ARTIE. *(Responding to a dismissive gesture from Dorothea.)* Thank you.

DOROTHEA. Don't mention it. *(Lights fade on Dorothea and Echo. They exit.)*

ARTIE. I have trouble with my memory. It can't forget. Anything. My social security number; poems I learned twenty years ago; the list of ingredients in Raisin Bran; what I weighed when I was twelve; what my mother *said* about what I weighed. Every word I've ever read. Everything I've seen, or heard, or was part of. *(Taps her forehead.)* It's all up here. Total recall. There are people who'd be grateful for it, I suppose. To me, it's like I'm some sort of ... memorial. with all the names of the dead etched in. No way to erase. *(A beat.)* I try not to read much anymore. Don't want to make the memorial any bigger. *(A beat.)* My daughter — Echo — sometimes thinks I'm against education. I'm not against education. I'm just against remembering what you learn.

ECHO. Cathexis. C-A-T-H-E-X-I-S. Cathexis.

ARTIE. *(Softly, registering it for all time.)* Cathexis.

ECHO. *(Off.)* Plein-air. P-L-E-I-N hyphen A-I-R. Plein-air.

ARTIE. Plein-air.

ECHO. *(Off.)* Deodand. D-E-O-D-A-N-D. Deodand.

ARTIE. Deodand — these aren't words, they're fragments. Greek, Latin, Old French, Old German — they're parts of something we *used* to speak. They're sediment, they're...

ECHO. *(Off.)* Detritus. D-E-T-R-I-T-U-S. Detritus.

ARTIE. Echo. I have to hang up now.

ECHO. *(Off.)* Can't we do a few more?

ARTIE. I have to hang up.

ECHO. *(Off.)* Are you all right?

ARTIE. I'm fine.

ECHO. *(Off.)* Really?

ARTIE. Really. *(A beat.)*

ECHO. *(Off.)* Goodbye.

ARTIE. Goodbye. *(To audience.)* My mother made sure I had tutors from the age of four. I remembered everything they ever said, of course — which excited them tremendously. Meanwhile my father worried that too much learning would hurt my hopes for marriage. But Dorothea told him a smart girl can hide what she knows, so there's still a chance for happiness. *(Lights up on Dorothea, seated a little way off. She breaks in, addressing the audience.)*

DOROTHEA. Well, that's true in a way...

ARTIE. I'm telling this. *(Turning again to audience.)* When I was eighteen, I got pregnant.

DOROTHEA. It was an accident...

ARTIE. Mother. *(Dorothea falls silent.)* In fourteen years of tutoring, no one — including my mother — ever brought up the facts of life. I knew the whole succession of Midianite kings, but I didn't know anything about the men who cut our lawn. 'Til I went out with one of them.

DOROTHEA. *(Rising suddenly into the scene, playing to an eighteen-year-old Artie.)* You can't be pregnant! You can't! You're eighteen.

176

ARTIE. Mother, I am.

DOROTHEA. You're about to go to *college.*

ARTIE. I can't help that.

DOROTHEA. Of course you can. Your college career...

ARTIE. What college career? I'm going to be a mother.

DOROTHEA. No. No, you're not. You don't have to be.

ARTIE. Of course I have to...

DOROTHEA. No. You don't. Think about it. *(A beat.)*

ARTIE. What — you mean give it up for adoption?

DOROTHEA. No. That would mean your father finding out. If he knew about this, he'd have you married to someone in five minutes — and no college, either. You have to do something else.

ARTIE. What? *(A beat, as it comes to her.)* That's *illegal!*

DOROTHEA. In this state. But if you go...

ARTIE. No!

DOROTHEA. Artie...

ARTIE. I won't do that.

DOROTHEA. Why not?

ARTIE. It's a life. *(A beat.)*

DOROTHEA. *(Quiet, steadfast.)* It's that life or yours.

ARTIE. How can you say that?

DOROTHEA. *Think* a minute. If you keep it, none of our plans, none of your potential — do you see? You'll spend the next twenty years of your life trying to catch up with yourself. You won't be *you* anymore. You'll just be something a child needs.

ARTIE. What's wrong with that?

DOROTHEA. You could be more. Something *else.*

ARTIE. I don't want to be anything more.

DOROTHEA. You are. *(A beat.)* We can't help what God made us. If you hadn't been born the way you are, I could've waggled letters over you crib forever and nothing would have come of it. *(A beat.)* If you have a baby now, your father will think, "Fine. She's just a woman, like I said all along. I'll find her a husband." He will, too. And we won't be able to stop him. *(A beat.)* When a soldier in battle suddenly has to kill someone, we say that's all right. It's his

177

life or someone else's — that's the choice, no matter how regrettable. Well, you have a choice, too. Between living your life or someone else's. You only get to make that choice once. And you have to choose now. *(Lights fade on Dorothea. Artie addresses the audience.)*

ARTIE. I waited. A little while, anyway. But finally we crossed the state line, and ... *(A beat.)* I ran away right after that. Across three state lines. I lied about my age and got a job teaching at a private school. I think they were surprised at my interview. They asked what I taught, and I said, "What have you got?" Chemistry and ancient history, they said. I said I could do both. And I did. I taught kids who were ... my age. And they called me Miss. I spent my free time being delighted not to be around my mother, and wondering how she was.

DOROTHEA. *(Coming into the light.)* I was fine, that's how I was. I was speaking daily with Mr. Norman Sweet, of the Sweet Detective Agency. He was making excellent progress.

ARTIE. One afternoon, I came home from teaching, and my mother was sitting in my room.

DOROTHEA. It's small, isn't it?

ARTIE. No, it's large.

DOROTHEA. I like the view. You can see a steel plant.

ARTIE. It's nice out the other window.

DOROTHEA. Where would you like to eat this afternoon? *(A beat.)* Where do you normally eat? *(A beat.)* Remember the meals back home? Now *those* are...

ARTIE. Those are over with. We already ate those meals.

DOROTHEA. *(With sudden enthusiasm.)* Guess what I've been working on! I just started it. Go on — guess!

ARTIE. Mom...

DOROTHEA. A way to see through the Earth! You can, you know. It has to do with the mind bending light. There's nothing the mind can't bend. What's it like to teach here? Challenging?

ARTIE. It's a nice school...

DOROTHEA. A minnow is a nice fish.

ARTIE. You don't have to like it, ok!? I don't care if you like it.

178

DOROTHEA. It doesn't matter whether I like it or not. You're coming home. *(Suddenly fishing in her bag.)* Oh! Guess what I bought the other day. Guess. It's for you.

ARTIE. What?

DOROTHEA. This. It's a book.

ARTIE. I can see that. *(A beat. Dorothea holds it out temptingly, waggles it slightly. Artie fights her natural urge to examine any book.)*

DOROTHEA. It's in Latin. An 1857 edition of Ovid's *Metamorphoses*. Published in Rome. It's in very good shape. *(Artie takes the book.)*

ARTIE. It's beautiful.

DOROTHEA. Well, it was expensive enough. But then I know how much you love Ovid, with all those young girls of his running away from the gods, turning into cows and constellations and things.

ARTIE. *(Grudgingly.)* Thank you.

DOROTHEA. *(Taking the book back, paging through it.)* Don't thank me. You have the right to an intellectual life. I wonder if these girls were glad. After they'd been transformed into trees and reeds and whatever. There's something so stationary about a tree. Oh well, too late for them. *(She freezes. Artie speaks to audience.)*

ARTIE. I ran away again. On the way home. I crawled out the bathroom window of Matt's Hygienic Cafe. *(She takes the book out of Dorothea's hand.)* With the book. *(Artie moves a little way off, as lights fade on the exiting Dorothea.)* This time I moved very far away. And I stayed hidden. For a long time. *(All lights fade to black. In the darkness, without a pause, we hear Echo softly singing a lullabye, "The Night Will Never Stay." which begins Scene 3.\* Lights slowly rise on Echo and Dorothea D. Dorothea sits on the platform. Echo methodically raises and lowers Dorothea's outstretched arm. Therapy for the stroke victim. Dorothea, eyes closed, speaks as Echo's song ends.)*

\*See Special Note on copyright page.

179

# Scene 3

DOROTHEA. *(To audience.)* People wonder about me. I realize that. *(Opening her eyes.)* They don't say anything, of course — because of the money. My husband was very comfortable. He owned most of the state, by the time he died. He always treated me ... civilly. He didn't really know what to make of me, except a wife. Not long after Artie ran away the second time, he died. Cerebral hemorrhage — very sudden. I'm told he didn't feel it much. I know I didn't. That worried me for a time, not feeling anything about the death of my husband. But then I asked a few of my women friends whose husbands had died, and they said the same thing. So I decided it was common enough, and I shouldn't worry.

ECHO. Euphrasy. E-U-P-H-R-A-S-Y. Euphrasy. A plant. Also known as eyebright. *(She begins to raise and lower Dorothea's other arm.)* Bijouterie. B-I-J-O-U-T-E-R-I-E. Bijouterie. A jewel collection. *(To the audience.)* Words are my collection. They're like jewels no one takes out of the case. Rataplan.

DOROTHEA. *(Eyes closed, smiling, enjoying the word.)* Rataplan.

ECHO and DOROTHEA. *(Together.)* R-A-T-A-P-L-A-N.

ECHO. Rataplan. The sound or beating of a drum. My grandmother loved helping me with words.

DOROTHEA. You spell them wonderfully.

ECHO. I've lived with my grandmother almost all my life. She raised me. *(She kneels in front of Dorothea, exercises the arms in crossing patterns.)*

DOROTHEA. Life is a swift ascent, followed by an endless, dreamy, downward nutation.

ECHO. That means, "a nodding off."

DOROTHEA. One can only hope one has risen high enough, so that the sights on the way down will be worth the looking.

ECHO. This is what I imagine she thinks. *(Echo rises, stares at her a moment, then gives her a kiss on the forehead. Dorothea smiles. Echo exits into the darkness. Dorothea, eyes still closed, turns her head in the direction Echo left. She suddenly rises, moves in that direction.)*

DOROTHEA. I've found out how to talk to stones!

ECHO. *(Off.)* You have, haven't you? *(Artie enters, lies down on the platform, eyes closed. Dorothea watches as she does so.)*

DOROTHEA. Isn't she pretty? I'm not blind to good looks, you know. Beauty *and* intelligence. I thought I was a very lucky mother. *(Artie gives a low groan.)* She's dreaming. I'm in her dream. Do you want to know what I'm like in her dream? *(Dorothea makes a horrible face, clowning.)* She can't help it. It's not her fault, and it's not mine. It wasn't my mother's fault either, I suppose. We all try to be just right, just what the next one needs. And we never come close. *(She kisses Artie sweetly on the forehead. Artie grimaces in her sleep.)* I was an only child. After me, my mother couldn't have any more. As for my father — well, the only sentence of genuine interest he ever uttered about me was, "Is it a boy?". I became my mother's daughter, by default. It gave me such a feeling of worthlessness. It was like an asthma of the soul. I could never take a deep breath of who I was.

ARTIE. *(Staring at Dorothea.)* For years I had the same dream.

DOROTHEA. Mother didn't know what to say. Father only glowered.

ARTIE. I dreamed my mother found out where I'd moved.

DOROTHEA. Girls really *weren't* worth much then.

ARTIE. I'd find her in my room, like the first time.

DOROTHEA. Mother told me not to think about it.

ARTIE. I dreamed she burned my books. That somehow there was a little, self-contained fire.

DOROTHEA. But thinking was the only thing I felt confident doing.

ARTIE. She burned the pillows and chairs — just tossed them in.

DOROTHEA. I read every book I could find.

ARTIE. The curtains, my papers, my clothes...

DOROTHEA. I read for escape.

ARTIE. Stop throwing things! Stop it! They're mine!

DOROTHEA. I felt guilty. In those days a girl did.

ARTIE. Then she asked me to get in. The fire.

DOROTHEA. But I couldn't help myself. I felt like an addict.

ARTIE. No! No! Get out of my room! *Get out!*

DOROTHEA. *(After a beat.)* Can you imagine it? Feeling guilty for learning?

ARTIE. *(Quietly.)* And then she would disappear. Just ... disappear. And the room would be like it was, and I'd be alone again. Only I'd be awake. *(Lights fade out on Artie, who slowly exits in the darkness.)*

DOROTHEA. The day I graduated high school, my father smiled at me, and said he had a wonderful surprise — which turned out to be an arranged marriage between me and John Wesbrook. John was, I admit, a sort of boyfriend — and I had thought of marrying him, perhaps, in four years. But what I thought didn't concern my father. I said, "What about college?". And he said, "John's going directly into his father's business." "No, no — what about college for me," I said. My father just laughed. He laughed at the idea that I might prefer college to marriage. He laughed and laughed. *(Lights up on Echo.)*

ECHO. I think you can get stuck on pleasure, don't you? You can get so involved with something you like, that you don't move on to the next thing. Something you might like even more.

DOROTHEA. My father — and John too — made vague promises I could go to college sometime if only I'd get married now. On June 2nd I graduated high school; three weeks later I was married; two weeks later I was pregnant. John and I had three boys and a baby girl. I liked the girl.

ECHO. *(Rising.)* For example, I love my grandmother. But since her stroke...

DOROTHEA. After our third son was born, I asked John if I could go to college. He said no. I reminded him of his vague promises. He said that's what vague promises were for.

ECHO. Now there's only Mom. And face to face with Mom, it's ... harder.

DOROTHEA. Then I met a very strange person.

182

ECHO. So I come here, and talk to Dorothea, even though she can't hear me.

DOROTHEA. A very strange person indeed.

ECHO. I move her arms, do words, and ... pretend she's still here.

DOROTHEA. *(As lights fade on Echo.)* He was a guest at a summer party. This was in the forties. Normally our guests were financial types. But he was the friend of a friend, *and* he was a spiritualist. I'd always thought such people were weird, funereal sorts, but this was the happiest man I'd ever met. He talked to me for a long time about his investigations into the supernatural. He didn't make these eccentric journeys for any dark, compelling reasons. He simply enjoyed the possibility of an entirely different world within our reach. I asked if that didn't seem like escapism. He said he couldn't think of a better world to escape from. "Look around you," he said, "Don't you just itch to escape?". But what would my husband think, I wondered. And this man — as though he'd been reading my thoughts — said, "The best thing about it is, *no one holds an eccentric responsible.*" And suddenly a great breath of happiness went down into my lungs. "Eccentricity," I thought — *"What* a relief!". From that day on, I never felt the need to listen to a thing my husband said — or anyone else. *(Lights up on Artie.)*

ARTIE. My mother chose to be an eccentric. Like choosing to be a Lutheran, she said.

DOROTHEA. *(Starting to lie back on the platform.)* Eccentricity solved so many problems. I could stay a wife and mother, and still converse with the souls of animals.

ECHO. *(Off.)* My grandmother's girlhood diary is amazing. She knew everything, and she loved so many people. When she married, it stopped. Like she died or something.

DOROTHEA. *(Eyes closed.)* Eccentricity saved my life. It became my life. I thank God for it. For all the good — and the harm — that it has caused. *(The action carries directly into Scene 4, with Dorothea on the platform, Echo just above her and Artie standing.)*

# Scene 4

ARTIE. She can't hear you.
ECHO. Maybe she can.
ARTIE. I don't think so.
ECHO. She talks sometimes.
ARTIE. She does not.
ECHO. Kind of talking.
ARTIE. She grunts. Like an animal. *(A beat.)* I don't know why you keep coming here.
ECHO. She's my grandmother.
ARTIE. Does she recognize you? She doesn't recognize me. So then whose grandmother is she, I ask myself. Whose mother is she? *(A beat.)* If you can't remember who you're related to...
ECHO. She's yours and she's mine, so just stop talking. *(A beat.)*
ARTIE. If there was a God, he'd kill us outright.
ECHO. There is, so shut up. You didn't have to come here.
ARTIE. I wanted to see what you two did together.
ECHO. We just sit here! I open the drapes, I close the drapes! *(A beat.)*
ARTIE. The nurses will hear you.
ECHO. The nurses hear me all the time.
ARTIE. You yell a lot in here?
ECHO. I used to. You tend to quiet down in this place after awhile.
ARTIE. It's a very good hospital. They do a better job than we could. *(A beat.)* Why do you keep coming here?
ECHO. To see my mother. *(This visibly affects Artie. She starts to leave, stops.)*
ARTIE. Be home in time for dinner.
ECHO. I will. *(Artie exits. Lights go down on Dorothea as Echo addresses the audience.)* My mother left me when I was little. For a long time, I wasn't sure if she'd left, or just suddenly got a lot older. Or I wondered if there'd ever been a mother at all. Maybe it'd

184

always been my grandmother, and I was just confused. I really thought that. I used to ask Dorothea where my mother was, and she'd always say...

DOROTHEA. *(In the darkness.)* She just stepped out.

ECHO. She what?

DOROTHEA. She just stepped out, dear.

ECHO. When's she going to step back in? Grandma? Grandma? *(Lights crossfade to Artie.)* Later, when I was old enough, Grandma told me that Mom had gone into research, whatever that is.

DOROTHEA. *(As before.)* Research is a place where you can study for the rest of your life.

ECHO. Once, Mom called on the phone. *(On the phone, a seven-year-old.)* Hello?

ARTIE. *(Off.)* Oh — hello. Is your ... Is Dorothea there? *(A beat.)*

ECHO. Who's this?

ARTIE. *(Off.)* Let me talk with your mother.

ECHO. *(Hesitating, then.)* No. *(Lights up on Dorothea, sitting.)*

DOROTHEA. Who called, dear?

ECHO. Nobody.

DOROTHEA. I heard a phone ring.

ECHO. It was nobody. It was a dead person.

DOROTHEA. A dead person?

ECHO. Nearly dead. *(A beat.)*

DOROTHEA. Why don't you come and sit next to me? Hm? Come on. Come on, come on, come on, come on. *(Slowly, Echo does so.)* There. That's nice, isn't it?

ECHO. No.

DOROTHEA. *(Laughing good-naturedly.)* Yes, it is. Now let me ask you a question. Do you know why I named you Echo?

ECHO. So kids would laugh at me.

DOROTHEA. No, so you could give back to others what you find beautiful about them. So you could reflect what's lovely in others.

ECHO. Then you should've named me mirror.

DOROTHEA. Not just living people. People from the past. People we only know from what they wrote, or said. I want you to hear what people say — to sort out what's helpful and forgiving, and ... return that to them. Do you understand?

ECHO. No.

DOROTHEA. We're all talking, all the time — saying our thoughts, writing them down, sending them out like messages in a bottle. And we're never sure which messages have been found and which haven't. If you could ... reassure some people...

ECHO. Like my mother?

DOROTHEA. Not only her.

ECHO. But mostly.

DOROTHEA. Me too.

ECHO. You? Why you?

DOROTHEA. Everyone needs...

ECHO. Why you? I love you.

DOROTHEA. Of course you do, but...

ECHO. But what? *(A beat.)*

DOROTHEA. We all need forgiveness. *(Lights on them start to dim as Artie enters. They exit during her speech.)*

ARTIE. When I ran away the second time, I kept moving. I lived in eight different cities. I used four different names. Once, after about three years, I called. Mom?

DOROTHEA. *(Off.)* Yes?

ARTIE. It's me.

DOROTHEA. I know.

ARTIE. I'm all right. Are you still looking for me?

DOROTHEA. No.

ARTIE. And I hung up. I moved again the next day, just in case. But I knew she was telling the truth. Finally I went back to school on my own. Paid my own way selling suitcases — which I thought was ironic. We had one suitcase I used to hit with a hammer, to show how rugged it was. I used to hit the crap out of that suitcase, but it never broke. The hammer broke. After a few more years I called again. Mom?

DOROTHEA. *(Off.)* Yes.

ARTIE. I'm still all right.

DOROTHEA. That's nice, dear.

ARTIE. I'm going to have a baby.

DOROTHEA. Is this your way of telling me you're married?

ARTIE. Yes ... um, his name is Richard, and he's a professor of biochemistry. I'm assisting him.

DOROTHEA. I should say you are. How long have you been married?

ARTIE. A few months. I've finished grad school.

DOROTHEA. You have? That's wonderful. What in?

ARTIE. Biochem.

DOROTHEA. That's lovely. Will you do research then?

ARTIE. Yes.

DOROTHEA. Interesting research, I hope?

ARTIE. Oh, yes. Of course.

DOROTHEA. When's the baby due?

ARTIE. Six months.

DOROTHEA. I'll come and stay with you. Where do you live now?

ARTIE. Oh — you don't have to do that.

DOROTHEA. I want to.

ARTIE. I know, but...

DOROTHEA. What state do you live in? Just tell me that.

ARTIE. I don't think...

DOROTHEA. You'll need your mother if you're going to have a baby. What state?

ARTIE. *(After a beat.)* California.

DOROTHEA. Out there, eh? Well, I'll have to make some arrangements, but...

ARTIE. Mom, don't come. I don't want you to.

DOROTHEA. Nonsense. I'll there in a week.

ARTIE. Mom...

DOROTHEA. What? *(Artie bows her head and sighs.)*

ARTIE. Don't you want to know what city I'm in?

DOROTHEA. No — I like the challenge.

ARTIE. A week later, there she was.

DOROTHEA. *(To audience.)* Hi!

ARTIE. She bought a house on our block. She came over every night. My husband actually liked her.

DOROTHEA. Richard had taste.

ARTIE. He had more than that. When I was with my husband, I had no memory at all — of where I came from, what I'd been like, or what I was afraid of. We worked together, loved each other. Every day was independent of other days. Each day was experienced and then put away — simply put away, as though it had been a whole life in itself. And every night was a ... quiet, lovely step ... from one life into another. *(A beat.)* When my mother arrived, my memory came back. Forever.

DOROTHEA. I like my new neighborhood. I saw King Solomon on the street yesterday, but he couldn't stop.

ARTIE. Richard didn't understand why I couldn't function with her around. I couldn't, though. She'd come over with some theory for making *toads fly,* and...

DOROTHEA. Don't get upset, dear. I'll be down the street when you need me.

ARTIE. When I had my baby, she took me to the hospital. My husband was at work. *(Dorothea mimes holding a baby in her arms. Her eyes shine.)*

DOROTHEA. A *girl. (Dorothea suddenly lifts the "baby" high above her.)*

ARTIE. *Mom!*

DOROTHEA. Oh, this one will fly. She'll fly. I can feel it.

ARTIE. Exactly one month after Echo was born, my husband died. In a car accident. As Dorothea put it...

DOROTHEA. *(Cradling the "baby.")* One death, one life — the world is always working like that.

ECHO. *(Entering.)* When my father died, Mom didn't talk for days. That's what Grandma said, anyway. Not even to ask for food or anything. I think she really loved him.

DOROTHEA. But...

ARTIE. As Dorothea put it...

DOROTHEA. I always say, the dead are the dead, and the living *are* the living.

ARTIE. That's not what you always say.

DOROTHEA. It's what I say at the moment. Now, how are we going to raise this child?

ARTIE. We?

DOROTHEA. You can't do it alone. You have a career to think of, you're aggrieved...

ARTIE. *I know I'm aggrieved.*

DOROTHEA. You see? I'll get my things and move in. We have work to do. *(Lights crossfade from these two to Echo. Beside her are the wings Artie wore in Scene 1. As she enters, she sings a short lullabye, "Rock Me To Sleep.")* *

ECHO. Grandma always sang lullabies to me. She sang them to my mother, too. I never heard my mother sing a word.

# Scene 5

*Lights grow brighter as Echo puts on the wings.*

ECHO. Like 'em? I do. Grandma never threw anything away, even things she was sorry for. I wish they'd worked. I wish Artie had flown. It's hard for Grandma — dedicating her life to theories that are ... difficult to prove. *(Moving D. with the wings, sitting.)* When I was a year old, the three of us moved back East, back into Grandma's house. We didn't fly, we drove. All the way across the country. I don't really remember that. *(Lights up on Dorothea.)*

DOROTHEA. I do. I wanted Echo to see a few things. We made all sorts of educational stops: a secret Indian burial ground, a convention of faith healers in Laramie, Wyoming, Edgar Cayce's birthplace, Edgar Cayce's grave, Edgar Cayce's wife's grave ... *(Lights up on Artie.)*

ARTIE. A voodoo cult in Louisiana, a "landing strip" for UFO's, and the home of a man who'd been to the moon and back — in

*See Special Note on copyright page.

189

1956. Our trip across the county took five weeks.

DOROTHEA. Echo saw things it took me years to see.

ARTIE. Echo saw things that weren't there.

ECHO. It must've been a nice trip. When we got back to Grandma's house, they put me in Mom's old room — though I wasn't aware of that at the time. *(Echo begins playing with the wings as though she were two years old. Artie and Dorothea sit U. watching her.)*

DOROTHEA. She's bright, isn't she?

ARTIE. You call chewing on a wing bright?

DOROTHEA. She already speaks Greek, a little.

ARTIE. She doesn't know what she's saying.

DOROTHEA. Yes, she does. Other people don't, but she does. Do you like your work these days?

ARTIE. Sure.

DOROTHEA. I know it's only teaching. But you'll get back to research someday. At least the college is close. That's the best thing about the East. There's always a college right down the street.

ARTIE. *(After a beat.)* I have a job offer.

DOROTHEA. Oh? In research?

ARTIE. Yes. Echo, stop chewing on those. *(Echo throws the wing down.)* Yes, I do.

DOROTHEA. Where is it? *(Echo unties her shoe, then tries to tie it again — unsuccessfully.)*

ARTIE. Europe.

DOROTHEA. Oh? *(A beat.)* For how long?

ARTIE. No limit.

DOROTHEA. Permanently?

ARTIE. If I want. Isn't that good news?

DOROTHEA. Well ... are you planning to take Echo with you? *(A beat.)* She'll grow up speaking a foreign language.

ARTIE. She already does. *(Echo raises the foot with the untied shoe and utters a foreign word.)*

ECHO. *Yah-yáh mou.*

DOROTHEA. *(To audience.)* The Greek word for "Grandma." *(Going to tie Echo's shoe.)* It's all right, I'm here. *(To Artie.)* She likes me. She's used to having me around. Almost more than you, I sometimes think.

ARTIE. What does that mean?

DOROTHEA. Nothing. I'm just ... observing. *(A beat.)* Echo.

ARTIE. *(Almost on top of Dorothea's line.)* Echo.

ECHO. *(Having untied her other shoe, waving her foot.)* Yah-yáh mou. *(Dorothea goes to tie it.)*

DOROTHEA. I was just observing. Are you sure you have to take this position?

ARTIE. It's the logical next step. *(A beat.)*

DOROTHEA. I'll come visit, then. What country is it in?

ARTIE. I don't want you to visit.

DOROTHEA. I have to come visit, I have to see Echo for one...

ARTIE. You can see her here. Every day. I want you to keep her.

DOROTHEA. Keep her? For how long?

ARTIE. For good. Echo. *(Echo raises her shoe, untied again.)*

ECHO. Yah-yáh mou.

ARTIE. I want you to keep her for good. *(Artie exits as light fades out on the area. Echo remains in a spot.)*

ECHO. Dorothea and I never talked about Artie much. Sometimes she'd bring out photographs though, and we'd have to. *(Lights up on Dorothea, with an album.)*

DOROTHEA. Echo, pictures! *(Echo moves beside her, sits. She is about six.)* I found a whole new album in the attic. It's got your mother in it.

ECHO. *(Unenthused.)* Ok.

DOROTHEA. This is Artie and I when we had those sessions with Mrs. Loreau. Here's a picture of Artie hypnotized.

ECHO. Hypnotized?

THEA. Oh yes. We used to get hypnotized quite regularly. We'd leave our bodies sometimes. At least, I would. It would be fun to do that with you, but I promised your mother we wouldn't.

ECHO. Why not?

191

DOROTHEA. Oh, here's a shot I like. It's Artie and I on a trip. I took her to one of those vortexes. You know, those houses where the balls roll up instead of down?

ECHO. No.

DOROTHEA. Well, they have them. And we went to see one. And the little ball rolled uphill, just like it was supposed to. I personally found a lot of strength in that, but Artie didn't like it at all. Your mother never found much pleasure in seeing the rules of the world broken. I knew they weren't being broken. There were just more rules than she thought there were.

ECHO. How many rules are there?

DOROTHEA. In the whole world?

ECHO. Yeah.

DOROTHEA. How many do you want? Because that's how many there'll be. *(She tweaks Echo's nose. Echo squeals. They freeze. Lights up slowly on Artie.)*

ARTIE. *(To audience.)* I still remember — I still remember everything but in particular I still remember being waked up by my mother, when I was seven. We sneaked out of the house late at night, just the two of us. It was late spring. The air was warm. My mother looked all excited. She pulled out...

DOROTHEA. *(Suddenly unfreezing, holding aloft the object she names.)* A pair of scissors.

ARTIE. *(As lights start to fade on the others.)* And she cut off a piece of my hair...

DOROTHEA. A *lock* of your hair...

ARTIE. *(As the others fade into darkness.)* A lock of my hair, and she said, "I will take this lock of hair, cut off in secret at the full moon, and I will save it as long as you are my daughter — whether we love each other or not, whether you remember me or forget me, whether I help you or harm you. I will always have it, till the day I die." *(Throughout the preceding speech, Dorothea's voice has gradually come up to join Artie's word for word. By the end of it, only Dorothea is speaking.)* And then we went home, and went back to bed. I asked her later where she kept my hair, but she wouldn't tell me.

DOROTHEA. *(In the dark.)* It's a secret. Even from you.

ARTIE. I just wanted to know. But no matter how much I begged

192

her, she wouldn't tell me.

DOROTHEA. *(As before.)* It's a terrible desire to want to know everything.

ARTIE. So one day, when she was gone, I looked. For five hours. I opened every drawer. I looked under every piece of furniture, in every pillow, under every rug, all through her jewelry collection, in the bathroom cabinets, *above* the bathroom cabinets. I checked the bottoms of drawers, the backs of drawers, the backs of furniture, behind mirrors, pictures...

DOROTHEA. *(As before.)* It's a terrible desire to want to know everything.

ARTIE. I stripped the sheets off her bed. I looked under the mattress, I looked through every book, every magazine, I felt in all her shoes, I looked behind the toilet, I felt on top of the doorframe...

DOROTHEA. *(As before.)* It's a terrible desire...

ARTIE. It wasn't anywhere! It wasn't anywhere in the *whole damn house!* *(A long beat. More quietly.)* When my mother got home, she found me sitting in a huge pile of her things on her bedroom floor. She didn't have to ask what I was doing. She went immediately to her dresser drawer, took out a small screwdriver, went to the light switch, unscrewed the plastic safety plate, and took out my lock of hair. And gave it to me.

DOROTHEA. *(As before.)* Here...

ARTIE. She said.

DOROTHEA. *(As before.)* You may keep it yourself. I don't want it anymore.

ARTIE. I was seven years old. *(A beat.)* I called up my mother once — from Europe — when Echo was seven. I had some news. *(Dorothea enters the light, stands right next to Artie. They speak to each other, but look directly at the audience.)*

DOROTHEA. Really? What is it?

ARTIE. I'm coming back. I have a job opportunity in the states. Close to you.

DOROTHEA. How close?

ARTIE. Fifty miles.

DOROTHEA. Well. That is close. Are you going to take it?

ARTIE. Yes.

DOROTHEA. When?

ARTIE. Soon. *(A beat.)*

DOROTHEA. Well. You know you're always welcome to visit. *(A beat.)*

ARTIE. I won't come visit.

DOROTHEA. Call then. You can call us anytime.

ARTIE. All right. *(A beat.)*

DOROTHEA. Do you want Echo back, or anything like that? *(A long beat.)*

ARTIE. No. *(Lights fade on Dorothea as Artie steps into a new area of light.)* My new job was a good one. It had a direct link-up with clinical research. We saved lives. Once I got settled in, I started to call my mother and Echo now and then. I'd ask Echo about school...

ECHO. *(Off.)* Probability Theory's interesting. I'll be able to do more with it when I'm nine.

ARTIE. And I'd ask Dorothea about her ... life.

DOROTHEA. *(Off.)* Last night I was assumed bodily into heaven.

ARTIE. Things went on this way for ... six years, actually. And in that whole time, I never saw Echo. *(A low spot comes up on Echo.)*

ECHO. Once you did.

ARTIE. *(Picking up a book.)* Well, once — yes. By accident. I was at a bookfair. I didn't go to buy books, really. I just went to ... hold them. I was running my hand over the spine of an eighteenth century early edition, wishing I could smell the book more than read it, and ... *(Seeing Echo across the stage.)* I saw her. She was a long way away, but I knew it was her — Dorothea'd sent me pictures. But pictures don't move. She was beautiful. *(Echo looks in Artie's direction.)* Just then she saw me. I immediately dropped the book and ran. I ran and ran, all the way to my car. I don't even remember driving home. *(Artie exits, leaving the book.)*

ECHO. *(Moving to pick the book up.)* I bought it. *Robinson Crusoe, The Life And Strange, Surprizing Adventures.* I read it seventeen times. *(Lights crossfade to Artie, in another area.)*

ARTIE. *(To audience.)* I think a woman has a right to be irrational about her children. Once she has them, she has them. They're hers. She thinks so, her husband thinks so, everyone thinks so. They came out of her body — they are her body. And anytime they want love, they can demand it. As long as she can open an eye, she'll see them. As long as she can hear a sound, it'll be them. Forever, from the moment they're born. The same is true for the one I didn't have. Only that one comes to me in my sleep, and asks for her love then. Echo calls me a bad mother. But if she could see me at night — how good I am then, how much care I take. *(Lights crossfade to Dorothea, who lies on the platform.)*
DOROTHEA. *(Raising one arm, running her hand over it.)* It really is an amazing thing, old age. Look at my skin. It's like the last layer of tissue paper, before you open a gift. *(Lights down on Dorothea.)*

# Scene 6

*Lights up on Echo.*

ECHO. Not long after that Mom suggested spelling bees. It was probably her way to apologize for running away from me that time. It got pretty important, though. She ended up calling me a lot more. *(Artie appears. She mimes cooking as she speaks on the phone. She carries a dictionary.)*
ARTIE. I'll find one, I'll find one. Just a minute. *(Paging through the dictionary.)* "Metamorphosis." You know that one, huh? Ok, how about ... "syllepsis?" You know *that?* Well, no, all right. Um ... "paronymous." *(Listening, nodding.)* Um-hm, um-hm, good. That's right. Now, let's — oh, damn! What? No, I just dropped the damn book, that's all. I'm trying to get dinner ready, and ... No, no, don't call back. Really. Don't. Stay on. I'm fine.

35

195

ECHO. I think she liked helping me. She spent a lot of time on it.

ARTIE. What do you mean that's not a hard one? "Oppugun" is a hard one. Spell it.

ECHO. *(Dutifully.)* Oppugn. O-P-P-U-G-N. Oppugn.

ARTIE. Fine.

ECHO. It was strange suddenly talking to her so much.

ARTIE. How was school today?

ECHO. Fine. They want me to take some college courses.

ARTIE. You're only thirteen.

ECHO. Gotta start sometime. How's work?

ARTIE. Fine. We're seeing some nice results with that new anticoagulant drug.

ECHO. *You're* seeing?

ARTIE. Well, we hear back. Oh, damn!

ECHO. What?

ARTIE. Dropped the peas.

ECHO. I should call back.

ARTIE. No, they're frozen — stay on the line.

ECHO. What are you working on now?

ARTIE. The potatoes.

ECHO. No, at work.

ARTIE. Oh — something with a carrot extract. Looks pretty positive. You want another word?

ECHO. Once, right in the middle of a conversation, I asked her why she left me. No warning. I just asked her. All she could say was...

ARTIE. You want another word? *(Lights fade on Artie.)*

ECHO. I decided I was going to get Mom to the National Spelling Bee finals. She'd said about a million times that she wasn't going, but I didn't care. I knew I was was going to be there, 'cause no one could beat me, and I knew Dorothea was coming. I wanted them both in the audience when I won it. I didn't care if they were on opposite sides of the room. I just wanted them both to see that I was the very best in the whole country. That no matter what they'd done — no matter how they'd done it — they'd produced in the end someone that was completely ... all right. Someone with perspective. P-E-R-S-P-E-C-T-I-V-E. Perspective.

ARTIE. *(From the dark.)* I don't think I really can, honey...

ECHO. Why not?

ARTIE. Things at the lab...

ECHO. Screw the lab.

ARTIE. Watch your language.

ECHO. Put little covers on your petri dishes and come. *(A beat.)*

ARTIE. No. I mean, I don't think I can.

ECHO. You don't want to.

ARTIE. It's not that...

ECHO. What is it?

ARTIE. Honey...

ECHO. Mom, if you aren't there, and if you don't come up and congratulate me after I win, *and* say hello to Grandma, *and* kiss her ... you can forget about ever calling me again. *(A beat.)* And I hung up. *(Echo smiles.)* She came. *(She exits as lights crossfade to Dorothea.)*

DOROTHEA. They held it in a big room, with lots and lots of lights and cameras and reporters. Reporters from all over — each one following a child from their own region. Lots of children, too. All of whom looked nervous. All except Echo. *(Lights back up on Artie.)*

ARTIE. Echo looked ... wonderful.

DOROTHEA. She had no trouble at all in the early going — spelling words that were, I take it, English.

ARTIE. All the kids were good, but only Echo had no fear at all. I couldn't see my mother. I knew she was somewhere in the room, but ... *(Lights suddenly up on Echo, her eyes closed in intense concentration.)*

ECHO. Glunch. G-L-U-N-C-H. Glunch. *(She opens her eyes, looks anxious, then smiles. She speaks quickly.)* I knew I was right. Glunch is such an easy word — spelled like it sounds. But you always have that little moment of doubt that maybe you *thought* the right letter, but you said the ... *(Interrupting herself.)* What's he getting? What's his word?

DOROTHEA. At last it came down to only Echo and a little boy.

ECHO. *Donzel?!* That's so easy! Why didn't I get that? I know it — donzel, unknighted gentleman.

ARTIE. The boy looked very nervous.

ECHO. I should've had donzel. It's not fair. *(Suddenly outraged.)* He guessed! He guessed and he *got it!* That dumb shit! He didn't know it and he guessed. I could kill him! *(Suddenly her public self.)* Yes, Ma'am, I'm ready. *(Listens for the word she must spell.)* Palinode? *(A huge grin on her face, as once again we hear her thoughts.)* Palinode — great! I love that word. That's the easiest word there is. Thank God! Thank God — I deserve it. I've had too many hard words, and he's guessed on too many. Palinode — a poem in which a poet takes back something he said in another poem. *(Public again.)* Palinode. P-A-L-I-N-O-D-E. Palinode. *(Again she looks anxious until she receives confirmation that she is right. Her grin is almost totally malicious.)* This can't go on forever, buddy. I'm going to crack you like an egg.

ARTIE. Echo was a little different than I thought she'd be. I mean, she was terrific and everything, but she seemed so ... desperate.

DOROTHEA. She was frightening, is what she was. More frightening than anyone I can remember. Oh, Hitler and Mussolini were worse, certainly, but from them you expected it.

ECHO. What's his word? What's his word? I bet I know his word — what is it? Ovoviviparousness? I *know* that! I know it. It's the quality of being ovoviviparous. Why'd *he* get it?!

DOROTHEA. I knew Artie might come. I wondered what she would think.

ECHO. He's guessing! I know he's guessing! Dear God, please let me win! Please! I want five minutes. Just five minutes when all the lights are on me, and all the pictures are being taken of me, and for five minutes I'm the most famous child in America, and Mom and Dorothea see it! After that you can wash me back into the ocean with everybody else. I don't care. I'll just be one of the rabble, hoi polloi, the clamjamfry, the ... *(Her public self again.)* What? Excuse me, could you repeat the word? *Clamjamfry? (Overjoyed.)* I don't believe it! She asked the exact word I was thinking of! *(With machine-gun precision.)* Clamjamfry. C-L-A-M-J-A-M-F-R-Y. Clamjamfry. *(Awed by her own abilities.)* I know *everything in the world!!!*

ARTIE. I didn't know why she was behaving that way, so competitive. I mean, that's good to be, but ... not *too* much.

ECHO. *(With total disdain.)* Zonule. Look, at him — he's so proud he knew a word. Zonule. Everybody knows that.

DOROTHEA. I remembered when Artie had first suggested the Spelling Bee. I didn't like the idea. "Why do that?" I said, "If you already know the word, why beat someone to death with the fact? I mean, is that what I raised her for?"

ECHO. *(With great intensity.)* Come on, miss it! You don't know it. You know you don't. I do. I know how to spell it, I know what it means, I know its derivation, I know its earliest use in literature, I know its ... *(Her eyes widen. Her voice is a whisper of awe.)* He missed it!

DOROTHEA. When the boy missed the word, his little head collapsed — just collapsed down on his chest. As though it were on hinges. Echo didn't notice. She was looking at the woman who gave the words. Echo's eyes were as wide as an owl's. Not the "wise old owl" — not that at all. No, more like the real one. The one that hunts.

ECHO. Eleemosynary. E-L-E-E-M-O-S-Y-N-A-R- *(To the boy, with killer instinct.)* Y. *(Echo's reaction is that of the winner. Her arms start to rise in a triumphant gesture. Her face radiates joy. She freezes.)*

DOROTHEA. I could only watch the little boy. He just stood there. Cameras were going off, people were cheering and shaking Echo's hand — but the boy never moved. And his head stayed on his chest. His neck — figuratively at least — was broken.

ARTIE. I slowly made my way to the front of the room. Echo was being mobbed, but all I could look at was the boy she'd beaten. He looked like a dead mouse.

ECHO. The kid's mom made him congratulate me — he seemed almost like an old person. I don't think he ever thought he could lose. Now he was looking at sixty more years in his life he didn't know what to do with. *(A beat.)* Mom and Grandma got to the stage at the same time. But by then I'd been shoved over to the side for an interview. I couldn't hear what they said.

ARTIE. *(By now next to Dorothea, raising her voice due to the "crowd.")* Hello. Congratulations.

DOROTHEA. For what?

ARTIE. For Echo. For her doing so well.

DOROTHEA. Doing what?

ARTIE. Spelling.

DOROTHEA. Oh, I see. Artie, I must tell you, I grew very tired of the Spelling Bee, so I transformed it into a ballroom dance.

ARTIE. A what?

DOROTHEA. A ballroom dance. In my mind. I'm using telemutation. Right now you're dancing with an admiral.

ARTIE. Mother...

DOROTHEA. As soon as things settle down, I'll change it all back again, and we'll go home.

ARTIE. Mother, I have to do something...

DOROTHEA. What?

ARTIE. I have to kiss you.

DOROTHEA. What?!

ARTIE. I have to kiss you, so Echo can see. Hi, Echo!

ECHO. *(From a distance.)* Hi!

DOROTHEA. It'll look odd, two women kissing at a ballroom dance ... *(Artie quickly kisses her, waves again at Echo.)*

ARTIE. Congratulations, honey! I'll call soon! *(She starts to make her way out.)*

ECHO. Mom! Wait!

ARTIE. I'll call.

ECHO. Grandma, make her stay! Mom!

ARTIE. Goodbye!

ECHO. Mom! *Mom! (But she is gone.)* Grandma!

DOROTHEA. *(Shrugging, calling to Echo.)* She left with the

admiral! *(Lights fade to black.)*

# Scene 7

*In the darkness, we hear Echo singing a lullabye, "The Telephone Book Lullabye."\* Lights rise slowly.*

ECHO. *(Suddenly stopping.)* Eleemosynary. That's the one I won with. Means "charitable." I used it like a weapon, though. I thought having both of them there would be a good thing. But it wasn't. It made me realize that I was just like them. No better. I wasn't any end-product. I wasn't any ... less cruel. I was just a very intelligent, vicious person. *(A beat.)* I called Mom a few times after the Spelling Bee. She was always civil, but ... she was different. I stopped calling after awhile. For two years we hardly talked at all. Then one morning, Dorothea had a stroke. So Mom came home. *(Lights up on Artie as Echo begins emptying a drawer — mimed. Artie moves toward her.)*

ARTIE. I don't have to take your room.

ECHO. It's your room. At least, it used to be.

ARTIE. What about the other rooms? There's Dorothea's room.

ECHO. *No one* sleeps in there. That's hers. She might come back.

ARTIE. She won't come back.

ECHO. She might. Or don't you believe in miracles?

ARTIE. Do you?

ECHO. No one sleeps in there!

ARTIE. All right. But why do you want me in this room?

ECHO. 'Cause I can't be in it anymore. There's too many good memories of Grandma and me. I never want to come in here again. I want to freeze it in my mind, just like it was.

\*See Special Note on copyright page.

201

ARTIE. And that's why you want me in it? So you never have to come in the room I'm in?

ECHO. *(Finishing with the drawer.)* I'll be right down the hall. *(Echo starts to exit.)*

ARTIE. I don't expect you to like me. *(A beat.)* I'm going to stay.

ECHO. You don't know *what* you're going to do. *(She exits. Lights crossfade from Artie to Dorothea, who is doing some simple exercises.)*

DOROTHEA. I exercised every day of my life — right up until the stroke. That was all right, though. I'd lived a good while already. And I was planning to do a lot of research once I was dead. Life was interesting, from what I saw of it. I once asked Artie what she thought life was. You know what she said? "A long apology." Can you imagine? I said, "No, no, Artie — not *your* life. Life in general." She hung up. Of course. Poor Artie could never answer me back. Or anyone else, for that matter. *(A beat, as she sits on the platform.)* I thought Echo would be the one to preoccupy my thoughts in the last year or two of life. But it wasn't her. It was Artie. *(With fascination, lying back.)* Imagine. It was Artie. *(By now she is lying down, eyes closed. Artie and Echo appear. They sit.)*

ECHO. We were both asleep in chairs when she died. The nurse came in and found us like that. Must've looked like mass suicide. She woke up Artie first, and told her.

ARTIE. *(In a dim light, slowly "waking," listening.)* Thank you. *(Light fades out on Dorothea.)*

ECHO. *(With a smile.)* The next day, Mom and I had our first real fight.

ARTIE. *(Rising, in the rising light.)* It started over the wings.

ECHO. She wanted to burn them.

ARTIE. I didn't think that was so unreasonable.

ECHO. I found out she'd been burning things all morning. Anything that was evidence of Dorothea's eccentricity. Like she'd been a witch or something.

ARTIE. *(Into the argument by now.)* I'm not saying she was a witch...

ECHO. Then what are you saying?

ARTIE. Will you just give me the wings?

ECHO. I can't believe you burned all those things. You even burned her *books.*

ARTIE. For God's sake, they were books on levitation.

ECHO. They were hers!

ARTIE. *They aren't anymore! (A beat. She takes the wings from Echo.)* I just don't want her to be ... ridiculed, that's all. Her memory. People will be coming. Relatives. For the the funeral.

ECHO. Just put these things away, then. They won't be looking all through the house.

ARTIE. Of course they will. It's her estate. They inherit things too. My brothers are all coming.

ECHO. When?

ARTIE. Tomorrow, some of them. They're looking forward to seeing you.

ECHO. I don't even remember them.

ARTIE. They remember you.

ECHO. We could put Grandma's things in the garage. We could put them under something...

ARTIE. Your Uncle Bill is bringing his whole family — his wife and two girls.

ECHO. What if we did that? What if we put things in the garage?

ARTIE. The girls are just a little older than you.

ECHO. What are we going to do with Grandma's things?!

ARTIE. *I don't care! (A beat.)* I think you'll like your Uncle Bill. He was always my favorite brother. They have a very nice family. *(A beat.)* They'd ... they'd like you to live with them.

ECHO. What?

ARTIE. They say they'd be very pleased if you went to live with them.

ECHO. Whose idea was that?

ARTIE. Mine. *(A beat.)* They're a very normal family.

ECHO. I don't want a normal family.

ARTIE. I'd be bad for you. I've always been bad for you.

ECHO. You have not.

ARTIE. You could try it for just awhile...

ECHO. No. You said you were staying.

ARTIE. I was wrong. I thought I could, but...

ECHO. What's wrong with me?

ARTIE. Nothing.

ECHO. Then why do you keep leaving me!?

ARTIE. Echo...

ECHO. *Why!? (A beat. Artie sits tiredly.)*

ARTIE. I used to teach you wrong things. Do you know that?

ECHO. What do you mean? When?

ARTIE. When you were little. When Dorothea was with you every day, waggling those ... goddamn letters and cooing. You loved it, of course. You with your superhuman attention span. The two of you got along great. *(Sighs.)* So I taught you wrong things.

ECHO. Wrong things?

ARTIE. I taught you wrong names for things. When you were starting to talk. I'd point at the floor and say, "ceiling." I'd point at the door and say, "window." And you'd smile and say ceiling and window, and I began to hope if I could just ... retard you a little...

ECHO. *Retard* me...?!

ARTIE. Just a little — just to be normal. I thought if you didn't seem so bright, she might get disinterested and leave us alone. But she didn't. She noticed you were "mixed up" on one or two concepts. So she sneaked around until she heard me telling you your hands were your feet. She accused me of "intellectual child abuse." That sounds ridiculous, but it was true. I actually was angry at you. For picking her. For wanting her more.

ECHO. I wanted you both.

ARTIE. You couldn't have both. You got her. She was better for you than I could've been.

ECHO. Do you really believe that? *(A beat.)* Do you?

ARTIE. Yes. *(A beat.)*

ECHO. How long do you want me to live with Uncle Bill and ... the girls? *(A silence. Echo picks up the wings.)* I'm taking these. I'm taking everything of Grandma's that ... I'm taking everything.

ARTIE. *(Quietly.)* All right. *(Echo starts out, stops.)*

ECHO. Did you love me? When you left me with her?

ARTIE. Echo...

ECHO. Did you?

ARTIE. Whether I loved you then or now...

ECHO. *Did you love me? Do you?*

ARTIE. *Yes.* And no. It's always yes and no. *(They regard each other. Echo exits. Lights fade on Artie, rise on Echo in another area.)*

ECHO. My cousin's names were Whitney and Beth. I sat between them in the car the whole way home. It was obvious they'd been told to be nice to me. They asked about my clothes. They said they loved them, and wanted to know where I got them. I said I didn't know. Then it was quiet for awhile. Then Beth asked, "Where did you buy those wings?" — but Uncle Bill broke right in and said, "Your mother is very well thought of in her field. You should be proud of her." Then it was quiet for about a hundred miles. Then Whitney said, "If you want, you can wear my clothes." Then we were home. *(Lights crossfade to Artie.)*

ARTIE. I moved out of my old room and into Dorothea's room. The next day, I moved from Dorothea's room to a guest room. A couple days later, I moved down to a sleeping porch. That was a little better. I planned to go back home after a week or two of ... tying things up. But the day before I left I turned around and ... *(Lights up on Echo a few feet away. She is without the wings.)*

ECHO. Hello.

ARTIE. What are you doing here?

ECHO. All my stuff's in the hall. Where do you want me to put it?

ARTIE. Where's your Uncle Bill? Where's...?

ECHO. I left them.

ARTIE. Why?

ECHO. I don't know. We were all at one of Whitney and Beth's lacrosse games and I just ... left.

ARTIE. I'll go call them.

ECHO. Tell them I'm staying here.

ARTIE. You are not staying here. *(A beat. They stare at each other.)* You are not.

ECHO. You said you loved me.

ARTIE. I said yes and no.

ECHO. But that means sometimes you love me. Sometimes you do, don't you?

ARTIE. Echo...

ECHO. *Sometimes you do.* And if I work on it enough, I can get you to love me more of the time. *Most* of the time.

ARTIE. *(Turning to go.)* I'm calling your Uncle Bill.

ECHO. Uncle Bill hardly remembers you, you know that? I asked him what you were like as a little girl, and he couldn't even say. He remembers Grandma even less. He didn't have one interesting story about her — about *Grandma.* They don't have a single picture of her, either. Not even in their minds. To them, she's just a woman who lived a big, embarrassing life. They all think they've saved me just in time. Not just from Grandma — from you, too.

ARTIE. They never said that.

ECHO. They don't have to. *(A beat.)* So I started wondering if they weren't right. Maybe the smartest thing would be to forget you completely. And Grandma. After all, what did I ever get from the two of you, except a good education? You especially — what were you ever to me, except a voice on the phone now and then? And I looked around the new room where I was staying, and it was real nice and ... blank, the way a thing is before you put any time into it. I thought, I could live a whole new life here. I could invent a whole new me. I could be Barbara if I wanted to, not Echo. I could fit in. I don't mean I'd become like Whitney and Beth. I'm not that crazy. But I could become like Robinson Crusoe, and adapt myself to a strange and harsh environment. I could live in a kind of desert. I could even flourish. Like you have. I could live without the one thing I wanted. But I kept hearing your voice. That voice on the phone, hiding behind spelling words, making excuses — or so energetic sometimes, so ... wishing. I don't even remember what you said, just the sound of it. Just a sound that said, "I love you, and

206

I failed you." I hate that sound. And I will never settle for it, because no one failed me. No one ever failed me. Not Grandma and not you. I am a prize among women. I'm your daughter. That's what I choose to be. Someone who loves you. Someone who can make you love me. Nearly all the time. I'm going to stay with you. I'm going to prepare you for me. I'm going to cultivate you. I'm going to tend you.

ARTIE. *(Quietly.)* Do you think I'm a garden?

ECHO. Yes. And you need work. *(Echo holds out her hand to Artie. Lights crossfade to Dorothea.)*

DOROTHEA. It's fascinating, being dead. Really, I find it's all in how you approach a thing. Take me — I've just begun a project searching for life after eternity. So far, it's going very well. *(Lights crossfade to Artie, now alone.)*

ARTIE. We kept the wings. We even kept the movie. Echo makes me watch it now and then. She tries to point out what's positive in it. I must admit, she tries very hard. She made me promise not to leave her. I'm one person who can't forget a promise. *(Lights up on Echo.)*

ECHO. I love to watch that movie. To see them both together, speaking and moving.

DOROTHEA. *(From the darkness.)* Today I am going to prove that man — or in this case, woman — can fly without the aid of any motor of any kind.

ECHO. She was right, too. I've almost got Mom believing it. You know what I sometimes think about the Wesbrook women? That no matter what we've done — no matter how we've done it — we're all three of us, in our own way, completely ... eleemosynary. *E-L-E-E-M-O-S-Y-N-A-R-Y* "Charitable; the giving of alms." *(Lights fade quickly to black.)*

## THE END